INSIGHT  GUIDES

SPANISH

PHRASEBOOK & DICTIONARY

T0124465

Contacting the Editors
Every effort has been made to provide accurate information in this publication, but changes are inevitable. The publisher cannot be responsible for any resulting loss, inconvenience or injury. We would appreciate it if readers would call our attention to any errors or outdated information. We also welcome your suggestions; if you come across a relevant expression not in our phrase book, please contact us at: **hello@insightguides.com**

All Rights Reserved
© 2015 Apa Digital (CH) AG and Apa Publications (UK) Ltd

First Edition: 2015
Printed in China

Cover & Interior Design: Pawel Pasternak
Production: AM Services
Production Manager: Vicky Glover
Picture Researcher: Slawek Krajewski
Cover Photo: all iStockphoto

Interior Photos: all iStockphoto

CONTENTS

FOOD & DRINK

GOING OUT

DICTIONARY

PRONUNCIATION

On the following pages and throughout the book, you will find
our simplified phonetic system in italics. This will help you learn
to pronounce Spanish easily. While this section is only intended
as a guide, it should provide you with the necessary basics to
help you to start speaking and be understood. Simply read the
pronunciation as if it were English.

Please note that underlined letters indicate that a syllable
should be stressed. The acute accent ´ also indicates stress, e.g.
río, _ree_-oh. Some Spanish words have more than one meaning.
In these instances, the accent mark is also used to distinguish
between them, e.g.: **sí** (yes) and **si** (if).

For a more in-depth look at the pronunciation, look at the tables
that follow.

You will also notice that some words are followed by an _m_ or an
_f_; these denote masculine and feminine versions. Choose the
one that is appropriate for the situation. Remember also that
feminine nouns take feminine adjectives and so forth.

CONSONANTS

Letter	Approximate Pronunciation	Symbol	Example	Pronunciation
b	1. as in English	b	**bueno**	_bweh • noh_
	2. between vowels as in English, but softer	b	**bebida**	_beh • bee • dah_
c	1. before e and i like th in thin	th	**centro**	_thehn • troh_
	2. otherwise like k in kit	k	**como**	_koh • moh_
ch	as in English	ch	**mucho**	_moo • choh_
d	1. as in English	d	**donde**	_dohn • deh_
	2. between vowels and especially at the end of a word, like th in thin, but softer	th	**usted**	_oos • teth_
g	1. before e and i, like ch in Scottish loch	kh	**urgente**	_oor • khehn • teh_
	2. otherwise, like g in get	g	**ninguno**	_neen • goo • noh_
h	always silent		**hombre**	_ohm • breh_
j	like ch in Scottish loch	kh	**bajo**	_bah • khoh_
ll	like y in yellow	y	**lleno**	_yeh • noh_
ñ	like ni in onion	ny	**señor**	_seh • nyohr_
q	like k in kick	k	**quince**	_keen • theh_
r	trilled, especially at the beginning of a word	r	**río**	_ree • oh_
rr	strongly trilled	rr	**arriba**	_ah • rree • bah_
s	1. like s in same	s	**sus**	_soos_
	2. before b, d, g, l, m, n, like s in rose	z	**mismo**	_meez • moh_
v	like b in bad, but softer	b	**viejo**	_beeyeh • khoh_
z	like th in thin	th	**brazo**	_brah • thoh_

Letters f, k, l, m, n, p, t, w, x and y are pronounced as in English.

VOWELS

Letter	Approximate Pronunciation	Symbol	Example	Pronunciation
a	like the a in father	**ah**	**gracias**	*grah • theeyahs*
e	like e in get	**eh**	**esta**	*ehs • tah*
i	like ee in meet	**ee**	**sí**	*see*
o	like o in rope	**oh**	**dos**	*dohs*
u	1. like oo in food	**oo**	**uno**	*oo • noh*
	2. silent after g and q		**que**	*keh*
	3. when marked ü, like we in well	**w**	**antigüe-dad**	*ahn • tee • gweh • dahd*
y	1. like y in yellow	**y**	**hoy**	*oy*
	2. when alone, like ee in meet	**ee**	**y**	*ee*
	3. when preceded by an a, sounds like y + ee, with ee faintly pronounced	**aye**	**hay**	*aye*

ⓘ

With over 400 million Spanish speakers worldwide, Spanish is the third most widely spoken language in the world and the official language of 21 different nations. Over 17 million people in the United States speak Spanish as their native language, and it is one of the official languages of the United Nations. Below are the estimated numbers of Spanish speakers around the globe.

Central America: 55 million
North America: 112 million
South America: 190 million
Spain: 40 million

HOW TO USE THE APP

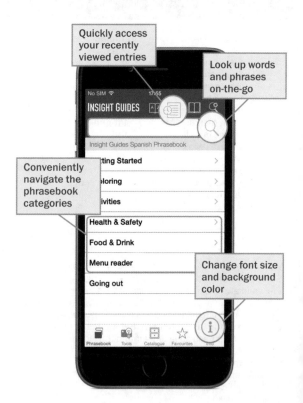

Quickly access your recently viewed entries

Look up words and phrases on-the-go

Conveniently navigate the phrasebook categories

Change font size and background color

Save the most useful everyday words and phrases to your Favorites

Use the Flash Cards Quiz to learn and memorize new words easily

Insight Guides Spanish Phrasebook

Can you recommend a good restaurant/ bar?
¿Puede recomend... ... buen

restaurante/bar?
_pweh•deh reh•koh•meh... dahr•meh
oon bwehn rehs•taw•rahn•teh/bahr_

Take all digital advantages of the app: listen to words and phrases pronounced by native speakers

Is there a t...

Phrasebook   Tools   Catalogue   Favourites   Info

To learn how to Activate the app, see the inside back cover of this phrasebook.

THE BASICS

GRAMMAR

In Spanish, there are a number of forms for 'you' (taking different verb forms): **tú** (singular) and **vosotros** *m*/**vosotras** *f* (plural) are used when talking to relatives, close friends and children; **usted** (singular) and **ustedes** (plural) are used in all other cases. If in doubt, use **usted/ustedes**. The following abbreviations are used in this section: Ud. = Usted; Uds. = Ustedes; sing. = singular; pl. = plural; inf. = informal; for. = formal.

REGULAR VERBS

There are three verb types that follow a regular conjugation pattern. These verbs end in **–ar**, **–er** and **–ir**. Following are the present, past and future forms of the verbs **hablar** (to speak), **comer** (to eat) and **vivir** (to live). The different conjugation endings are in bold.

HABLAR		Present	Past	Future
I	**yo**	habl**o**	habl**é**	hablar**é**
you (sing.)	**tú**	habl**as**	habl**aste**	hablar**ás**
he/she/you	**él/ella/Ud.**	habl**a**	habl**ó**	hablar**á**
we	**nosotros**	habl**amos**	habl**amos**	hablar**emos**
you (pl.)	**vosotros** *m* **vosotras** *f*	habl**áis**	habl**asteis**	hablar**éis**
they/you	**ellos/ellas/ Uds.**	habl**an**	habl**aron**	hablar**án**

COMER		Present	Past	Future
I	**yo**	com**o**	com**í**	comer**é**
you (sing.)	**tú**	com**es**	com**iste**	comer**ás**
he/she/you	**él/ella/Ud.**	com**e**	com**ió**	comer**á**

we	nosotros	comemos	comimos	comeremos
you (pl.)	vosotros *m*	coméis	comisteis	comeréis
	vosotras *f*			
they/you	ellos/ellas/ Uds.	comen	comieron	comerán

VIVIR		Present	Past	Future
I	yo	vivo	viví	viviré
you (sing.)	tú	vives	viviste	vivirás
he/she/you	él/ella/Ud.	vive	vivió	vivirá
we	nosotros	vivimos	vivimos	viviremos
you (pl.)	vosotros *m*	vivís	vivisteis	viviréis
	vosotras *f*			
they/you	ellos/ellas/ Uds.	viven	vivieron	vivirán

IRREGULAR VERBS

In Spanish, there are many different irregular verbs; these aren't conjugated by following the normal rules. The two most commonly used, and confused, irregular verbs are **ser** and **estar**. Both verbs mean 'to be', but are used in different contexts (see page 14). Following are the past, present and future tenses of **ser** and **estar** for easy reference.

SER	Present	Past	Future
yo	soy	fui	seré
tú (sing.)	eres	fuiste	serás
él/ella/Ud.	es	fue	será
nosotros	somos	fuimos	seremos
vosotros *m*	sois	fuisteis	seréis
vosotras *f* (pl.)			
ellos/ellas/Uds.	son	fueron	serán

ESTAR	Present	Past	Future
yo	estoy	estuve	estaré
tú (sing.)	estás	estuviste	estarás
él/ella/Ud.	está	estuvo	estará
nosotros	estamos	estuvimos	estaremos
vosotros *m*	estáis	estuvisteis	estaréis
vosotras *f* (pl.)			
ellos/ellas/Uds.	están	estuvieron	estarán

Ser is used to describe a fixed quality or characteristic. It is also used to tell time and dates.

Example: **Yo soy estadounidense.** I am American.

Here **ser** is used because it is a permanent characteristic.

Estar is used when describing a physical location or a temporary condition.

Example: **Estoy cansado.** I am tired.

Here **estar** is used because being tired is a temporary condition.

WORD ORDER

In Spanish, the conjugated verb comes after the subject.

Example: **Yo trabajo en Madrid.** I work in Madrid.

To ask a question, reverse the order of the subject and verb, change your intonation or use key question words such as **cuándo** (when).

Examples: **¿Cuándo cierra el banco?** When does the bank close?

Literally translates to: 'When closes the bank?' Notice the order of the subject and verb is reversed; a question word also begins the sentence.

¿El hotel es viejo? Is the hotel old?

Literally, the hotel is old. This is a statement that becomes a question by raising the pitch of the last syllable of the sentence.

NEGATIONS

To form a negative sentence, add **no** (not) before the verb.
Example: **Fumamos.** We smoke.
No fumamos. We don't smoke.

IMPERATIVES

Imperative sentences, or sentences that are a command, are
formed by adding the appropriate ending to the stem of the
verb (i.e. the verb in the infinitive without the **-ar**, **-er**, **-ir** ending).
Example: Speak!

you (sing.) (inf.)	tú	¡Habla!
you (sing.) (for.)	Ud.	¡Hable!
we	nosotros	¡Hablemos!
you (inf.)	vosotros	¡Hablad!
you (pl.) (for.)	Uds.	¡Hablen!

NOUNS & ARTICLES

Nouns are either masculine or feminine. Masculine nouns usually
end in **–o**, and feminine nouns usually end in **–a**. Nouns become
plural by adding an **–s**, or **–es** to nouns not ending in **–o** or **–a**
(e.g. **tren** becomes **trenes**). Nouns in Spanish get an indefinite
or definite article. An article must agree with the noun to which it
refers in gender and number. Indefinite articles are the equivalent
of 'a', 'an' or 'some' in English, while definite articles are the
equivalent of 'the'.
Indefinite article examples: **un tren** *m* (a train); **unos trenes** *m*
(some trains)**; una mesa** *f* (a table); **unas mesas** *f* (some tables)
Definite examples: **el libro** *m* (the book); **los libros** *m* (the books);
la casa *f* (the house); **las casas** *f* (the houses)
A possessive adjective relates to the gender of the noun that
follows and must agree in number and gender.

	Singular	Plural
my	mi	mis
your (sing.)	tu	tus
his/her/its/your	su	sus
our	nuestro *m*/nuestra *f*	nuestros *m*/nuestras *f*
your (pl.)	vuestro *m*/vuestra *f*	vuestros *m*/vuestras *f*
their/your	su	sus

Examples: **¿Dónde está <u>tu</u> chaqueta?** Where is your jacket?
<u>Vuestro</u> vuelo sale a las ocho. Your flight leaves at eight.

ADJECTIVES

Adjectives describe nouns and must agree with the noun in gender and number. In Spanish, adjectives usually come after the noun. Masculine adjectives generally end in −o, feminine adjectives in −a. If the masculine form ends in −e or with a consonant, the feminine form is generally the same. Most adjectives form their plurals the same way as nouns.
Examples: **Su hijo *m*/hija *f* es simpatico *m*/simpatico *f*.** Your son/daughter is nice.
El mar *m*/La flor *f* es azul. The ocean/The flower is blue.

COMPARATIVES & SUPERLATIVES

The comparative is usually formed by adding **más** (more) or **menos** (less) before the adjective or noun. The superlative is formed by adding the appropriate definite article (**la/las**, **el/los**) and **más** (the most) **menos** (the least) before the adjective or noun.

Example:

grande	**más grande**	**el m más grande** **la f más grande**
big	bigger	biggest
caro m/cara f	**menos caro m/cara f**	**el m/la f menos** **caro m/cara f**
expensive	less expensive	least expensive

POSSESSIVE PRONOUNS

Pronouns serve as substitutes for specific nouns and must agree with the noun in gender and number.

	Singular	Plural
mine	**mío m/mía f**	**míos m/mías f**
yours (inf.)	**tuyo m/tuya f**	**tuyos m/tuyas f**
yours	**suyo m/suya f**	**suyos m/suyas f**
his/her/its	**suyo m/suya f**	**suyos m/suyas f**
ours	**nuestro m/nuestra f**	**nuestros m/** **nuestras f**
yours (inf.)	**vuestro m/vuestra f**	**vuestros m/** **vuestras f**
theirs	**suyo m/suya f**	**suyos m/suyas f**

Example: **Ese asiento es mío.** That seat is mine.

ADVERBS & ADVERBIAL EXPRESSIONS

Adverbs are used to describe verbs. Some adverbs are formed by adding **-mente** to the adjective.
Example: **Roberto conduce lentamente.** Robert drives slowly.
The following are some common adverbial time expressions:
actualmente presently
todavía no not yet
todavía still
ya no not anymore

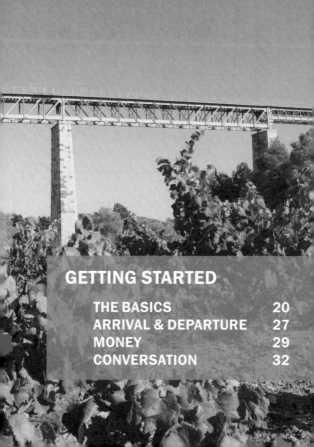

GETTING STARTED

THE BASICS

NUMBERS

0	**cero**	
	theh • roh	
1	**uno**	
	oo • noh	
2	**dos**	
	dohs	
3	**tres**	
	trehs	
4	**cuatro**	
	kwah • troh	
5	**cinco**	
	theen • koh	
6	**seis**	
	seyees	
7	**siete**	
	seeyeh • teh	

8	**ocho**
	_oh_ • choh
9	**nueve**
	nweh • beh
10	**diez**
	deeyehth
11	**once**
	ohn • theh
12	**doce**
	doh • theh
13	**trece**
	treh • theh
14	**catorce**
	kah • _tohr_ • theh
15	**quince**
	keen • theh
16	**dieciséis**
	deeyeh • thee • _seyees_
17	**diecisiete**
	deeyeh • thee • _seeyeh_ • teh
18	**dieciocho**
	deeyeh • thee • _oh_ • choh
19	**diecinueve**
	deeyeh • thee • _nweh_ • beh
20	**veinte**
	beyeen • teh
21	**veintiuno**
	beyeen • tee • _oo_ • noh
22	**veintidós**
	beyeen • tee • _dohs_
30	**treinta**
	treyeen • tah
31	**treinta y uno**

	treyeen • tah ee oo • noh
40	**cuarenta**
	kwah • rehn • tah
50	**cincuenta**
	theen • kwehn • tah
60	**sesenta**
	seh • sehn • tah
70	**setenta**
	seh • tehn • tah
80	**ochenta**
	oh • chehn • tah
90	**noventa**
	noh • behn • tah
100	**cien**
	theeyehn
101	**ciento uno**
	theeyehn • toh oo • noh
200	**doscientos**
	dohs • theeyehn • tohs
500	**quinientos**
	kee • neeyehn • tohs
1,000	**mil**
	meel
10,000	**diez mil**
	deeyehth meel
1,000,000	**un millón**
	oon mee • yohn

ORDINAL NUMBERS

first	**primero** *m*/**primera** *f*
	pree • meh • roh/pree • meh • rah
second	**segundo** *m*/**segunda** *f*
	seh • goon • doh/seh • goon • dah

Large numbers are read as in English. Example:
1,234,567 would be **un millón, doscientos treinta y cuatro mil, quinientos sesenta y siete** (one million, two hundred thirty-four thousand, five hundred sixty-seven).
Notice the use of **y** (and) between tens and units for numbers between 31 (**treinta y uno**; literally, thirty and one) and 99 (**noventa y nueve**; literally, ninety and nine).

third	**tercero** *m*/**tercera** *f*
	tehr • <u>theh</u> • roh/tehr • <u>theh</u> • rah
fourth	**cuarto** *m*/**cuarta** *f*
	<u>kwahr</u> • toh/<u>kwahr</u> • tah
fifth	**quinto** *m*/**quinta** *f*
	<u>keen</u> • toh/<u>keen</u> • tah
once	**una vez**
	<u>oo</u> • nah behth
twice	**dos veces**
	dohs <u>beh</u> • thes
three times	**tres veces**
	trehs <u>beh</u> • thes

TIME

NEED TO KNOW

What time is it?	**¿Qué hora es?**
	keh <u>oh</u> • rah ehs
It's noon [midday].	**Son las doce del mediodía.**
	sohn lahs <u>doh</u> • theh dehl meh • deeyoh • <u>dee</u> • ah
At midnight.	**A medianoche.**
	ah meh • deeyah • <u>noh</u> • cheh

From one o'clock to two o'clock.	**De una a dos en punto.**
	deh <u>oo</u> • nah ah dohs ehn <u>poon</u> • toh
Five after [past] three.	**Las tres y cinco.**
	lahs trehs ee <u>theen</u> • koh
A quarter to five.	**Las cinco menos cuarto.**
	lahs <u>theen</u> • koh meh • nohs <u>kwahr</u> • toh
5:30 a.m./p.m.	**Las cinco y media de la mañana/ tarde.**
	lahs <u>theen</u> • koh ee meh • deeyah deh lah mah • <u>nyah</u> • nah/<u>tahr</u> • deh

Spaniards use the 24-hour clock when writing time, especially in schedules. The morning hours from 1:00 a.m. to noon are the same as in English. After that, just add 12 to the time: 1:00 p.m. would be 13:00, 5:00 p.m. would be 17:00 and so on.

DAYS

NEED TO KNOW

Monday	**lunes**
	<u>loo</u> • nehs
Tuesday	**martes**
	<u>mahr</u> • tehs
Wednesday	**miércoles**
	<u>meeyehr</u> • koh • lehs
Thursday	**jueves**
	<u>khweh</u> • behs

Friday	**viernes**
	beeyehr • nehs
Saturday	**sábado**
	sah • bah • doh
Sunday	**domingo**
	doh • meen • goh

DATES

yesterday	**ayer**
	ah • yehr
today	**hoy**
	oy
tomorrow	**mañana**
	mah • nyah • nah
day	**día**
	dee • ah
week	**semana**
	seh • mah • nah
month	**mes**
	mehs
year	**año**
	ah • nyoh

MONTHS

January	**enero**
	eh • neh • roh
February	**febrero**
	feh • breh • roh
March	**marzo**
	mahr • thoh
April	**abril**
	ah • breel

May	**mayo**
	mah • yoh
June	**junio**
	khoo • neeyoh
July	**julio**
	khoo • leeyoh
August	**agosto**
	ah • gohs • toh
September	**septiembre**
	sehp • teeyehm • breh
October	**octubre**
	ohk • too • breh
November	**noviembre**
	noh • beeyehm • breh
December	**diciembre**
	dee • theeyehm • breh

SEASONS

the spring	**la primavera**
	lah pree • mah • beh • rah
the summer	**el verano**
	ehl beh • rah • noh
the fall [autumn]	**el otoño**
	ehl oh • toh • nyoh
the winter	**el invierno**
	ehl een • beeyehr • noh

HOLIDAYS

January 1: New Year's Day, **Año Nuevo**
January 6: Epiphany, **Epifanía**
February 8: Carnaval, **Carnaval**
March 19: Feast of St. Joseph, **San José**
May 1: Labor Day, **Día del Trabajo**

When different gender forms apply throughout this book, you will see the masculine version highlighted with an *m*; the feminine version with an *f*. Simply read the one that is appropriate for you. For example, on page 32, you say **Encantado** if you are a man; **encantada** if you are a woman.

July 25: Feast of St. James, **Santiago Apóstol**
August 15: Feast of the Assumption, **Asunción**
October 12: Spain's National Day, **Día de la Hispanidad**
November 1: All Saint's Day, **Todos los Santos**
December 6: Constitution Day, **Día de la Constitución**
December 8: Feast of the Immaculate Conception, **Inmaculada Concepción**
December 25: Christmas, **Navidad**
Easter is a moveable feast and dates vary each year.

ARRIVAL & DEPARTURE

NEED TO KNOW

I'm on vacation/ business.	**Estoy aquí de vacaciones/ en viaje de negocios.** *ehs • toy ah • kee deh bah • kah • theeyohn • ehs/ehn beeyah • kheh deh neh • goh • theeyohs*
I'm going to…	**Voy a…** *boy ah…*
I'm staying at the… Hotel.	**Me alojo en el Hotel…** *meh ah • loh • khoh ehn ehl oh • tehl…*

BORDER CONTROL

I'm just passing through.	**Estoy de paso.** ehs • <u>toy</u> deh <u>pah</u> • soh
I'd like to declare…	**Quiero declarar…** <u>keeyeh</u> • roh deh • klah • <u>rahr</u>…
I have nothing to declare.	**No tengo nada que declarar.** noh <u>tehn</u> • goh <u>nah</u> • dah keh deh • klah • <u>rahr</u>

YOU MAY HEAR…

Su pasaporte, por favor.
soo pah • sah • <u>pohr</u> • teh pohr fah • <u>bohr</u>
Your passport, please.

¿Cuál es el propósito de su visita?
kwahl ehs ehl proh • <u>poh</u> • see • toh
deh soo bee • <u>see</u> • tah
What's the purpose of your visit?

¿Dónde se aloja?
<u>dohn</u> • deh seh ah • <u>loh</u> • khah
Where are you staying?

¿Cuánto tiempo piensa quedarse?
<u>kwahn</u> • toh <u>teeyehm</u> • poh <u>peeyehn</u> • sah
keh • <u>dar</u> • seh
How long are you staying?

¿Con quién viaja?
kohn keeyehn <u>beeyah</u> • khah
Who are you here with?

YOU MAY SEE…

ADUANAS	customs
ARTÍCULOS LIBRES DE IMPUESTOS	duty-free goods
ARTÍCULOS QUE DECLARAR	goods to declare
NADA QUE DECLARAR	nothing to declare
CONTROL DE PASAPORTES	passport control
POLICÍA	police

YOU MAY HEAR...

¿Tiene algo que declarar?
teeyeh • neh ahl • goh keh deh • klah • rahr

Anything to declare?

Tiene que pagar impuestos por esto.
teeyeh • neh keh pah • gahr eem • pwehs • tohs pohr ehs • toh

You must pay duty on this.

Abra esta maleta.
ah • brah ehs • tah mah • leh • tah

Open this bag.

MONEY

NEED TO KNOW

Where's...?	**¿Dónde está...?** _dohn • deh ehs • tah..._
the ATM	**el cajero automático** _ehl kah • kheh • roh awtoh • mah • tee • koh_
the bank	**el banco** _ehl bahn • koh_
the currency exchange office	**la casa de cambio** _lah kah • sah deh kahm • beeyoh_
When does the bank open/close?	**¿A qué hora abre/cierra el banco?** _ah keh oh • rah ah • breh/theeyeh • rrah ehl bahn • koh_
I'd like to change dollars/pounds into euros.	**Quiero cambiar dólares/libras a euros.** _keeyeh • roh kahm • beeyahr doh • lah • rehs/lee • brahs ah ew • rohs_
I'd like to cash traveler's checks [cheques].	**Quiero cobrar cheques de viaje.** _keeyeh • roh koh • brahr cheh • kehs deh beeyah • kheh_

AT THE BANK

I'd like to change money/get a cash advance.	**Quiero cambiar dinero/ un adelanto de efectivo.** *keeyeh • roh kahm • beeyahr dee • neh • roh/oon ah • deh • lahn • toh deh eh • fehk • tee • boh*
What's the exchange rate?	**¿Cuál es el tipo de cambio?** *kwahl ehs ehl tee • poh deh kahm • beeyoh*
How much is the fee?	**¿Cuánto es la tasa?** *kwahn • toh ehs lah tah • sah*

YOU MAY SEE...

INTRODUCIR TARJETA AQUÍ	insert card here
CANCELAR	cancel
BORRAR	clear
INTRODUCIR	enter
CLAVE	PIN
RETIRAR FONDOS	withdraw funds
DE CUENTA CORRIENTE	from checking [current] account
DE CUENTA DE AHORROS	from savings account
RECIBO	receipt

I lost my traveler's checks.	**He perdido los cheques de viaje.** *eh pehr • dee • doh lohs cheh • kehs deh beeyah • kheh*
My card was lost.	**Se me ha perdido la tarjeta.** *seh meh ah pehr • dee • doh lah tahr • kheh • tah*
My card was stolen.	**Me han robado la tarjeta.** *meh ahn roh • bah • doh lah tahr • kheh • tah*

YOU MAY SEE…

Spanish currency is the **euro**, **€**, divided into 100 **céntimos** (cents).
Coins: 1, 2, 5, 10, 20, 50 cts.; €1, 2
Notes: €5, 10, 20, 50, 100, 200, 500

My card doesn't work.	**Mi tarjeta no funciona.**
	mee tahr•kheh•tah noh foon•theeyoh•nah
The ATM ate my card.	**El cajero automático se ha tragado mi tarjeta.**
	ehl kah•kheh•roh awtoh•mah•tee•koh seh ah trah•gah•doh mee tahr•kheh•tah

For Numbers, see page 20.

NEED TO KNOW

Hello!	**¡Hola!**
	_oh_ • lah
How are you?	**¿Cómo está?**
	koh • moh ehs • _tah_
Fine, thanks.	**Bien, gracias.**
	beeyehn _grah_ • theeyahs
Excuse me!	**¡Perdón!**
(to get attention)	pehr • _dohn_
Do you speak	**¿Habla inglés?**
English?	_ah_ • blah een • _glehs_
What's your name?	**¿Cómo se llama?**
	koh • moh seh _yah_ • mah
My name is…	**Me llamo…**
	meh _yah_ • moh…
Nice to meet you.	**Encantado** _m_/**Encantada** _f._
	ehn • kahn • _tah_ • doh/
	ehn • kahn • _tah_ • dah
Where are you from?	**¿De dónde es usted?**
	deh _dohn_ • deh ehs oos • _teth_

I'm from the U.S./U.K.	**Soy de Estados Unidos/ del ReinoUnido.**
	soy deh ehs • tah • dohs oo • nee • dohs/dehl reyee • noh oo • nee • doh
What do you do for a living?	**¿A qué se dedica?**
	ah keh seh deh • dee • kah
I work for…	**Trabajo para…**
	trah • bah • khoh pah • rah…
I'm a student.	**Soy estudiante.**
	soy ehs • too • deeyahn • teh
I'm retired.	**Estoy jubilado m/jubilada f.**
	ehs • toy khoo • bee • lah • doh/ khoo • bee • lah • dah
Do you like…?	**¿Le gusta…?**
	leh goos • tah…
Goodbye.	**Adiós.**
	ah • deeyohs
See you later.	**Hasta luego.**
	ah • stah lweh • goh

LANGUAGE DIFFICULTIES

Do you speak English?	**¿Habla inglés?**
	ah • blah een • glehs
Does anyone here speak English?	**¿Hay alguien que hable inglés?**
	aye ahl • geeyenh keh ah • bleh een • glehs
I don't speak (much) Spanish.	**No hablo (mucho) español.**
	noh ah • bloh (moo • choh) ehs • pah • nyol
Can you speak more slowly?	**¿Puede hablar más despacio?**
	pweh • deh ah • blahr mahs dehs • pah • theeyoh
Can you repeat that?	**¿Podría repetir eso?**
	poh • dree • ah reh • peh • teer eh • soh

> When you are greeting someone in Spain, you should use the appropriate greeting for the time of day. You can use the generic **hola** (hello) all day long; otherwise use **buenos días** (good morning) or **buenas tardes** (good afternoon/evening).

Excuse me?	**¿Cómo?** _koh • moh_
What was that?	**¿Qué ha dicho?** _keh ah dee • choh_
Can you spell it?	**¿Podría deletrearlo?** _poh • dree • ah deh • leh • treh • ahr • loh_
Please write it down.	**Escríbamelo, por favor.** _ehs • kree • bah • meh • loh pohr fah • bohr_
Can you translate this into English for me?	**¿Podría traducirme esto al inglés?** _poh • dree • ah trah • doo • theer • meh ehs • toh ahl een • glehs_
What does this/that mean?	**¿Qué significa esto/eso?** _keh seeg • nee • fee • kah ehs • toh/eh • soh_
I understand.	**Entiendo.** _ehn • teeyehn • doh_
I don't understand.	**No entiendo.** _noh ehn • teeyehn • doh_
Do you understand?	**¿Entiende?** _ehn • teeyehn • deh_

> When addressing strangers, always use the more formal **usted** (singular) or **ustedes** (plural), as opposed to the more familiar **tú** (singular) or **vosotros** (plural), until told otherwise. If you know someone's title, it's polite to use it, e.g., **doctor** (male doctor), **doctora** (female doctor). You can also simply say **Señor** (Mr.), **Señora** (Mrs.) or **Señorita** (Miss).

> **YOU MAY HEAR...**
> **Hablo muy poco inglés.**   I only speak
> _ah_ • bloh mooy _poh_ • koh een • _glehs_   a little English.
> **No hablo inglés.** noh _ah_ • bloh een • _glehs_   I don't speak
> English.

MAKING FRIENDS

Hello!
: **¡Hola!**
  _oh_ • lah

Good morning.
: **Buenos días.**
  bweh • nohs _dee_ • ahs

Good afternoon.
: **Buenas tardes.**
  bweh • nahs _tahr_ • dehs

Good evening.
: **Buenas noches.**
  bweh • nahs _noh_ • chehs

My name is...
: **Me llamo...**
  meh _yah_ • moh...

What's your name?
: **¿Cómo se llama?**
  koh • moh seh _yah_ • mah

I'd like to introduce you to...
: **Quiero presentarle a...**
  keeyeh • roh preh • _sehn_ • _tahr_ • leh ah...

Pleased to meet you.
: **Encantado** _m_/**Encantada** _f._
  ehn • kahn • _tah_ • doh/ehn • kahn • _tah_ • dah

How are you?
: **¿Cómo está?**
  koh • moh ehs • _tah_

Fine, thanks. And you?
: **Bien gracias. ¿Y usted?**
  beeyehn _grah_ • theeyahs ee oos • _tehth_

TRAVEL TALK

I'm here...
: **Estoy aquí...**
  ehs • _toy_ ah • _kee_...

on business	**en viaje de negocios**
	ehn _beeyah_ • kheh deh neh • _goh_ • theeyohs
on vacation	**de vacaciones**
	deh bah • kah • _theeyoh_ • nehs
studying	**estudiando**
	ehs • too • _deeyahn_ • doh
I'm staying for…	**Voy a quedarme…**
	boy ah keh • _dahr_ • meh…
I've been here…	**Llevo aquí…**
	yeh • boh ah • kee…
a day	**un día**
	oon _dee_ • ah
a week	**una semana**
	_oo_ • nah seh • _mah_ • nah
a month	**un mes**
	oon mehs
Where are you from?	**¿De dónde es usted?**
	deh _dohn_ • deh ehs
	oos • _tehth_
I'm from…	**Soy de…**
	soy deh…

For Numbers, see page 20.

PERSONAL

Who are you with?	**¿Con quién ha venido?**
	kohn keeyehn ah beh • _nee_ • doh
I'm here alone.	**He venido solo m/sola f.**
	eh beh • _nee_ • doh soh • loh/_soh_ • lah
I'm with my…	**He venido con mi…**
	eh beh • _nee_ • doh kohn mee…
husband/wife	**marido/mujer**
	mah • _ree_ • doh/moo • _khehr_
boyfriend/	**novio/novia**
girlfriend	_noh_ • beeyoh/_noh_ • beeyah

friend	**amigo/amiga**
	ah-mee-goh/ah-mee-gah
friends	**amigos/amigas**
	ah • mee • gohs/ah-mee-gahs
colleague	**colega**
	koh • leh • gah
colleagues	**colegas**
	koh-leh-gahs
When's your birthday?	**¿Cuándo es su cumpleaños?**
	kwahn • doh ehs soo koom • pleh • ah • nyohs
How old are you?	**¿Qué edad tiene usted?**
	keh eh • dahth teeyeh • neh oos • tehth
I'm…	**Tengo…años.**
	tehn • goh…ah • nyohs
Are you married?	**¿Está casado m/casada f?**
	ehs • tah kah • sah • doh/kah • sah • dah
I'm…	**Estoy…**
	ehs • toy…
single	**soltero m/soltera f**
	sohl • teh • roh/sohl • teh • rah
in a relationship	**en una relación**
	ehn oo • nah reh • lah • theeyohn

engaged	**comprometido** m/**comprometida** f
	kohm • proh • meh • tee • doh/
	kohm • proh • meh • tee dah
married	**casado** m/**casada** f
	kah • <u>sah</u> • doh/kah • <u>sah</u> • dah
divorced	**divorciado** m/**divorciada** f
	dee • bohr • <u>theeyah</u> • doh/
	dee • bohr • <u>theeyah</u> • dah
separated	**separado** m/**separada** f
	seh • pah • <u>rah</u> • doh/seh • pah • <u>rah</u> • dah
I'm widowed.	**Soy viudo** m/**viuda** f
	soy <u>beeyoo</u> • doh/<u>beeyoo</u> • dah
Do you have children/ grandchildren?	**¿Tiene hijos/nietos?**
	<u>teeyeh</u> • neh <u>ee</u> • khohs/<u>neeyeh</u> • tohs

For Numbers, see page 20.

WORK & SCHOOL

What do you do for a living?	**¿A qué se dedica?**
	ah keh seh deh • <u>dee</u> • kah
What are you studying?	**¿Qué estudia?**
	keh ehs • <u>too</u> • deeyah
I'm studying Spanish.	**Estudio español.**
	ehs • <u>too</u> • deeyoh ehs • pah • <u>nyohl</u>
I…	**Yo…**
	yoh…
work full-time/ part-time	**trabajo a tiempo completo/parcial**
	trah • <u>bah</u> • khoh ah <u>teeyehm</u> • poh kohm • <u>pleh</u> • toh/pahr • <u>theeyahl</u>
am unemployed	**estoy en el paro**
	ehs • <u>toy</u> ehn ehl <u>pah</u> • roh
work at home	**trabajo desde casa**
	trah • <u>bah</u> • khoh dehs • deh <u>kah</u> • sah
Who do you work for?	**¿Para quién trabaja?**
	<u>pah</u> • rah keeyehn trah • <u>bah</u> • khah

I work for…	**Trabajo para…**
	trah • bah • khoh pah • rah…
Here's my business card.	**Aquí tiene mi tarjeta.**
	ah • kee teeyeh • neh mee tahr • kheh • tah

For Social Media, see page 84.

WEATHER

What's the forecast?	**¿Cuál es el pronóstico del tiempo?**
	kwahl ehs ehl proh • nohs • tee • koh dehl teeyehm • poh
What beautiful/terrible weather!	**¡Qué tiempo más bonito/feo hace!**
	keh teeyehm • poh mahs boh • nee • toh/feh • oh ah • theh
It's cool/warm.	**Está fresco/cálido.**
	esh • tah frehs • koh/kah • lee • doh
It's cold/hot.	**Hace frío/calor.**
	ah • theh free • oh/kah • lohr
It's rainy/sunny.	**Está lluvioso/soleado.**
	ehs • tah yoo • beeyoh/soh/soh • lee • ah • doh
It's snowy/icy.	**Hay nieve/hielo.**
	aye neeyeh/beh/eeyeh • loh
Do I need a jacket/an umbrella?	**¿Necesito una chaqueta/un paraguas?**
	neh • theh • see • toh oo • nah chah • keh • tah/oon pah • rah • gwahs

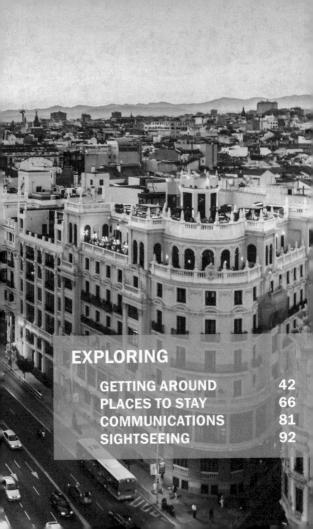

EXPLORING

GETTING AROUND

NEED TO KNOW

How do I get to town?	**¿Cómo se llega a la ciudad?** _koh • moh seh yeh • gah ah lah theew • dahd_
Where's...?	**¿Dónde está...?** _dohn • deh ehs • tah..._
the airport	**el aeropuerto** _ehl ah • eh • roh • pwehr • toh_
the train [railway] station	**la estación de tren** _lah ehs • tah • theeyohn deh trehn_
the bus station	**la estación de autobuses** _lah ehs • tah • theeyohn deh awtoh • booses_
the metro station	**la estación de metro** _lah ehs • tah • theeyohn deh meh • troh_
Is it far from here?	**¿A qué distancia está?** _ah keh dees • tahn • theeyah ehs • tah_
Where do I buy a ticket?	**¿Dónde se compra el billete?** _dohn • deh seh kohm • prah ehl_

	bee • yeh • teh
A one-way/return-trip ticket to…	**Un billete de ida/ida y vuelta a…**
	oon bee • yeh • teh deh ee • dah/ ee • dah ee bwehl • tah ah…
How much?	**¿Cuánto es?**
	kwahn • toh ehs
Is there a discount?	**¿Hacen descuento?**
	ah • then dehs • kwehn • toh
Which…?	**¿De qué…?**
	deh keh…
gate	**puerta de embarque**
	pwehr • tah deh ehm • bahr • keh
line	**línea**
	lee • neh • ah
platform	**andén**
	ahn • dehn
Where can I get a taxi?	**¿Dónde puedo coger un taxi?**
	dohn • deh pweh • doh koh • khehr oon tah • xee
Take me to this address.	**Lléveme a esta dirección.**
	yeh • beh • meh ah ehs • tah dee • rek • theeyohn
Where's the car hire?	**¿Dónde está el alquiler de coches?**
	dohn • deh ehs • tah ehl ahl • kee • lehr deh koh • chehs
Can I have a map?	**¿Podría darme un mapa?**
	poh • dree • ah dahr • meh oon mah • pah

TICKETS

When's…to Madrid?	**¿Cuándo sale…a Madrid?**
	kwahn • doh sah • leh…ah mah • dreeth
the (first) bus	**el (primer) autobús**
	ehl (pree • mehr) awtoh • boos

the (next) flight	**el (próximo) vuelo**
	ehl (<u>proh</u> • xee • moh) <u>bweh</u> • loh
the (last) train	**el (último) tren**
	ehl (<u>ool</u> • tee • moh) trehn
Where do I buy a ticket?	**¿Dónde se compra el billete?**
	<u>dohn</u> • deh seh kohm • prah ehl bee • <u>yeh</u> • teh
One/Two ticket(s), please.	**Un/Dos billete(s), por favor.**
	oon/dohs bee • <u>yeh</u> • teh(s) pohr fah • <u>bohr</u>
For today/tomorrow.	**Para hoy/mañana.**
	<u>pah</u> • rah oy/mah • <u>nyah</u> • nah
A…ticket.	**Un billete…**
	oon bee • <u>yeh</u> • teh…
one-way	**de ida**
	deh <u>ee</u> • dah
return-trip	**de ida y vuelta**
	deh <u>ee</u> • dah ee <u>bwehl</u> • tah
first class	**de primera clase**
	deh pree • <u>meh</u> • rah klah • she
business class	**de clase preferente**
	deh <u>klah</u> • seh preh • feh • <u>rehn</u> • teh
economy class	**de clase económica**
	deh <u>klah</u> • seh eh • koh • <u>noh</u> • mee • kah
How much?	**¿Cuánto es?**
	<u>kwahn</u> • toh ehs
Is there a discount for…?	**¿Hacen descuento a…?**
	<u>ah</u> • thehn dehs • <u>kwehn</u> • toh ah…
children	**los niños**
	lohs <u>nee</u> • nyohs
students	**los estudiantes**
	lohs ehs • too • <u>deeyahn</u> • tehs
senior citizens	**los jubilados**
	lohs khoo • bee • <u>lah</u> • dohs
tourists	**los turistas**
	too • <u>rees</u> • tahs

The express bus/ express train, please.	**El autobús exprés/tren exprés, por favor.** *ehl awtoh • boos/trehn ex • presh, pohr fah • bohr*
The local bus/ train, please.	**El autobús/tren local, por favor.** *ehl awtoh • boos/trehn loh • kahl, pohr fah • bohr*
I have an e-ticket.	**Tengo un billete electrónico.** *<u>tehn</u> • goh oon bee • <u>yeh</u> • teh eh • lehk • <u>troh</u> • nee • koh*
Can I buy a ticket on the bus/train?	**¿Puedo comprar el billete a bordo del autobús/tren?** *<u>pweh</u> • doh kohm • <u>prahr</u> ehl bee • <u>yeh</u> • teh ah <u>bohr</u> • doh dehl awtoh • <u>boos</u>/trehn*
Do I have to stamp the ticket before boarding?	**¿Tengo que sellar el billete antes de embarcar?** *tehn • goh keh seh • yahr ehl bee • yeh • teh ahn • tehs deh ehm • bahr • kahr*
How long is this ticket valid?	**¿Cuál es la validez de este billete?** *kwahl ehs lah bah • lee • dehth deh ehs • teh bee • yeh • teh*
Can I return on the same ticket?	**¿Puedo volver con el mismo billete?** *pweh • doh bohl • behr kohn ehl meesh • moh bee • yeh • teh*

I'd like to…my reservation.	**Quiero…mi reserva.** <u>keeyeh</u> • roh…mee reh • <u>sehr</u> • bah
cancel	**cancelar** kahn • theh • <u>lahr</u>
change	**cambiar** kahm • <u>beeyahr</u>
confirm	**confirmar** kohn • feer • <u>mahr</u>

For Time, see page 23.

PLANE

How much is a taxi to the airport?	**¿Cuánto cuesta el trayecto en taxi al aeropuerto?** kwahn • toh <u>kwehs</u> • tah ehl trah • <u>yehk</u> • toh ehn <u>tah</u> • xee ahl ah • eh • roh • <u>pwehr</u> • toh
To…Airport, please.	**Al aeropuerto de…, por favor.** ahl ah • eh • roh • <u>pwehr</u> • toh deh…pohr fah • <u>bohr</u>
My airline is…	**Mi compañía aérea es…** mee kohm • pah • <u>nyee</u> • ah ah • <u>eh</u> • reh • ah ehs…

YOU MAY HEAR…

¿Con qué compañía aérea viaja? kohn keh kohm • pah • <u>nyee</u> • ah ah • <u>eh</u> • reh • ah beeyah • khah	What airline are you flying?
¿Nacional o internacional? nah • theeyoh • <u>nahl</u> oh een • tehr • nah • theeyoh • <u>nahl</u>	Domestic or international?
¿Qué terminal? keh tehr • mee • <u>nahl</u>	What terminal?

My flight leaves at…	**Mi vuelo sale a la/las…**
	mee <u>bweh</u> • loh <u>sah</u> • leh ah lah/lahs…
I'm in a rush.	**Tengo prisa.**
	tehn • goh pree • sah
Can you take an alternate route?	**¿Puede coger otro camino?**
	pweh • deh koh • <u>khehr oh</u> • troh kah • <u>mee</u> • noh
Can you drive faster/slower?	**¿Puede ir más deprisa/despacio?**
	pweh • deh eer mahs deh • <u>pree</u> • sah/ dehs • <u>pah</u> • theeyoh

CHECKING IN

Where's check-in?	**¿Dónde está el mostrador de facturación?**
	<u>dohn</u> • deh ehs • <u>tah</u> ehl mohs • trah • <u>dohr</u> deh fahk • too • rah • <u>theeyohn</u>
My name is…	**Me llamo…**
	meh <u>yah</u> • moh…
I'm going to…	**Voy a…**
	boy ah…
I have…	**Tengo…**
	tehn • goh

YOU MAY SEE…

LLEGADAS	arrivals
SALIDAS	departures
RECOGIDA DE EQUIPAJES	baggage claim
VUELOS NACIONALES	domestic flights
VUELOS INTERNACIONALES	international flights
MOSTRADOR DE FACTURACIÓN	check-in
FACTURACIÓN ELECTRÓNICA	e-ticket check-in
PUERTAS DE EMBARQUE	departure gates

one suitcase	**una maleta**
	_oo_ • nah mah • _leh_ • tah
two suitcases	**dos maletas**
	dohs mah • _leh_ • tahs
one piece of hand luggage	**una pieza de equipaje de mano**
	oo • nah peeyeh • thah deh
	eh • kee • pah • kheh deh mah • noh
How much luggage is allowed?	**¿Cuánto equipaje está permitido?**
	kwahn • toh eh • kee • _pah_ • kheh
	ehs • _tah_ pehr • mee • _tee_ • doh
Is that pounds or kilos?	**¿Son libras o kilos?**
	sohn lee • brahs oh kee • lohs
Which terminal/ gate?	**¿De qué terminal/puerta de embarque?**
	deh keh tehr • mee • _nahl_/_pwehr_ • tah
	deh ehm • _bahr_ • keh
I'd like a window/an aisle seat.	**Quiero un asiento de ventana/pasillo.**
	keeyeh • roh oon ah • _seeyehn_ • toh deh
	behn • _tah_ • nah/pah • _see_ • yoh
When do we leave/arrive?	**¿A qué hora salimos/llegamos?**
	ah keh _oh_ • rah sah • _lee_ • mohs/
	yeh • _gah_ • mohs
Is the flight delayed?	**¿Lleva retraso el vuelo?**
	yeh • bah reh • _trah_ • soh ehl _bweh_ • loh
How late?	**¿Cuánto retraso lleva?**
	kwahn • toh reh • _trah_ • soh yeh • bah

LUGGAGE

Where is/are…?	**¿Dónde está/están…?**
	dohn • deh ehs • _tah_/ehs • _tahn_…
the luggage carts [trolleys]	**los carritos para el equipaje**
	lohs kah • _rree_ • tohs pah • rah ehl eh •
	kee • _pah_ • kheh

YOU MAY HEAR...

¡Siguiente! | Next!
see • geeyehn • teh

Su pasaporte/billete, por favor. | Your passport/
soo pah • sah • pohr • teh/bee • yeh • teh | ticket, please.
pohr fah • bohr

¿Va a facturar el equipaje? | Are you checking
bah ah fahk • too • rahr ehl | in any luggage?
eh • kee • pah • kheh

Lleva exceso de equipaje. | You have excess
yeh • bah ehx • theh • soh deh | luggage.
eh • kee • pah • kheh

Eso es demasiado grande para equipaje | That's too large for
de mano. | a carry-on [to
eh • soh ehs deh • mah • seeyah • doh | carry on board].
grahn • deh pah • rah
eh • kee • pah • kheh deh mah • noh

¿Hizo las maletas usted? | Did you pack these
ee • thoh lahs mah • leh • tahs oos • teth | bags yourself?

¿Le entregó alguien algún paquete? | Did anyone
leh ehn • treh • goh ahl • geeyehn ahl • | give you
goon pah • keh • teh | anything to carry?

Vacíese los bolsillos. | Empty your
bah • thee • eh • seh lohs bohl • see • yohs | pockets.

Quítese los zapatos. | Take off your
kee • teh • seh lohs thah • pah • tohs | shoes.

Se está efectuando el embarque | Now boarding
del vuelo... | flight...
seh ehs • tah eh • fehk • too • ahn • doh
ehl ehm • bahr • keh dehl bweh • loh...

the luggage lockers	**las consignas automáticas**
	lahs kohn • seeg • nahs awtoh • mah • tee • kahs
the baggage claim	**la recogida de equipajes**
	lah reh • koh • khee • dah deh eh • kee • pah • khehs
My luggage has been lost.	**Han perdido mi equipaje.**
	ahn pehr • dee • doh mee eh • kee • pah • kheh
My luggage has been stolen.	**Me han robado el equipaje.**
	meh ahn roh • bah • doh ehl eh • kee • pah • kheh
My suitcase is damaged.	**Mi maleta ha sufrido daños.**
	mee mah • leh • tah ah soo • free • doh dah • nyohs

FINDING YOUR WAY

Where is/are…?	**¿Dónde está/están…?**
	dohn • deh ehs • tah/ehs • tahn…
the currency exchange	**la casa de cambio**
	lah kah • sah deh kahm • beeyoh
the car hire	**el alquiler de coches**
	ehl ahl • kee • lehr deh koh • chehs
the exit	**la salida**
	lah sah • lee • dah
the taxis	**los taxis**
	lohs tah • xees
Is there…into town?	**¿Hay…que vaya a la ciudad?**
	aye…keh bah • yah ah lah theew • dahd
a bus	**un autobús**
	on awtoh • boos
a train	**un tren**
	on trehn
a metro	**un metro**
	on meh • troh

TRAIN

Where's the train station?	**¿Dónde está la estación de tren?** *dohn • deh ehs • tah lah ehs • tah • theeyohn deh trehn*
How far is it?	**¿A qué distancia está?** *ah keh dees • tahn • theeyah ehs • tah*
Where is/are…?	**¿Dónde está/están…?** *dohn • deh ehs • tah/ehs • tahn…*
the ticket office	**el despacho de billetes** *ehl dehs • pah • choh deh bee • yeh • tehs*
the information desk	**el mostrador de información** *ehl mohs • trah • dohr deh een • fohr • mah • theeyohn*

Spain's major railway network **RENFE (Red Nacional de Ferrocarriles Españoles)** offers a variety of rail services, with express, local, national and international trains. You can purchase tickets or make reservations through the **RENFE** website or a travel agency, or at the station. For popular routes and peak travel times and holiday periods, it's best to purchase tickets in advance.

the luggage lockers	**las consignas automáticas** lahs kohn • _seeg_ • nahs awtoh • _mah_ • tee • kahs
the platforms	**los andenes** lohs ahn • _deh_ • nehs
Can I have a schedule [timetable]?	**¿Podría darme un horario?** poh • _dree_ • ah _dahr_ • meh oon oh • _rah_ • reeyoh
How long is the trip?	**¿Cuánto dura el viaje?** _kwahn_ • toh doo • rah ehl _veeyah_ • kheh
Is it a direct train?	**¿Es un tren directo?** ehs oon trehn dee • _rehk_ • toh
Do I have to change trains?	**¿Tengo que cambiar de trenes?** _tehn_ • goh keh kahm • _beeyahr_ deh _treh_ • nehs
Is the train on time?	**¿El tren va puntual?** ehl trehn bah poon • _tooahl_

DEPARTURES

Which track [platform] for the train to…?	**¿De qué andén sale el tren a…?** deh keh ahn • _dehn_ sah • leh ehl trehn ah…
Is this the track [platform]/train to…?	**¿Es éste el andén/tren a…?** ehs ehs • teh ehl ahn • _dehn_/trehn ah…
Where is track [platform]…?	**¿Dónde está el andén…?** _dohn_ • deh ehs • _tah_ ehl ahn • _dehn_…

YOU MAY HEAR...

¡Todos a bordo!
toh • dohs ah bohr • doh

All aboard!

Billetes, por favor.
bee • yeh • tehs pohr fah • bohr

Tickets, please.

Tiene que cambiar de tren en León.
teeyeh • neh keh kahm • beeyahr deh trehn ehn leh • ohn

You have to change at Léon.

Próxima parada: Madrid.
proh • xee • mah pah • rah • dah mah • dreeth

Next stop, Madrid.

Where do I change for...?	**¿Dónde tengo que cambiar para...?** *dohn • deh tehn • goh keh kahm • beeyahr pah • rah...*

For Asking Directions, see page 61.

ON BOARD

Can I sit here?	**¿Le importa si me siento aquí?** *leh eem • pohr • tah see meh seeyehn • toh ah • kee*
Can I open the window?	**Puedo abrir la ventana?** *pweh • doh ah • breer lah behn • tah • nah*
That's my seat.	**Ése es mi asiento.** *eh • seh ehs mee ah • seeyehn • toh*
Here's my reservation.	**Esta es mi reserva.** *ehs • tah ehs mee reh • sehr • bah*

BUS

Where's the bus station?	**¿Dónde está la estación de autobuses?** *dohn • deh ehs • tah lah ehs • tah • theeyohn deh awtoh • boo • sehs*

> The bus service in Spain is extensive. For local service within a town, you usually pay as you board the bus. The fare is generally a fixed price. In larger cities, bus tickets are interchangeable with subway tickets. **Un bono** (**metrobús** in Madrid), a ten-trip ticket, is the cheapest way to go. These tickets are available at newsstands, lottery-ticket shops and subway stations. When using the **bono** on a bus, make sure to validate your ticket by stamping it in the machine next to the driver as you board. Signal that you wish to get off by pushing a button, located throughout the bus; a sign will light up that says **parada solicitada** (stop requested).

How far is it?	**¿A qué distancia está?**
	ah keh dees • tahn • theeyah ehs • tah
How do I get to…?	**¿Cómo se llega a…?**
	koh • moh seh yeh • gah ah…
Is this the bus to…?	**¿Es éste el autobús a…?**
	ehs ehs • teh ehl awtoh • boos ah…
How many stops to…?	**¿Cuántas paradas hay hasta…?**
	kwahn • tahs pah • rah • dahs aye ahs • tah…
Can you tell me when to get off?	**¿Podría decirme cuándo me tengo que bajar?**
	poh • dree • ah deh • theer • meh kwahn • doh meh tehn • goh keh bah • khahr
Do I have to change buses?	**¿Tengo que hacer transbordo?**
	tehn • goh keh ah • thehr trahns • bohr • doh
Stop here, please!	**¡Pare aquí, por favor!** *pah • reh ah • kee pohr fah • bohr*

For Tickets, see page 43.

👁

YOU MAY SEE...

PARADA DE AUTOBUSES	bus stop
SUBIR/BAJAR	enter/exit
PICAR BILLETE	stamp your ticket

ⓘ

In Spain, there are **metro** (subway) systems in Madrid, Barcelona, Valencia and Bilbao. They are easy to use and reasonably priced. You can save money by buying various multi-trip tickets which can be purchased at **metro** stations. In larger cities, **metro** and bus tickets are interchangeable so you can use all modes of transport using the same ticket. To enter the subway system with a paper ticket, slip your ticket through the slot in the turnstile; remember to grab your ticket, which now has the date printed on it, so that you can pass through the turnstile. You will also need this in case of a ticket inspection to prove you have paid for your journey.

METRO

Where's the metro?	**¿Dónde está la estación de metro?**
	dohn • deh ehs • tah lah ehs • tah • theeyohn deh meh • troh
A map, please.	**Un plano, por favor.**
	oon plah • noh pohr fah • bohr
Which line for...?	**¿Qué línea tengo que coger para...?**
	keh lee • neh • ah tehn • goh keh koh • khehr pah • rah...
Which direction?	**¿Qué dirección?** *keh dee • rehk • theeyohn*
Do I have to transfer [change]?	**¿Tengo que hacer transbordo?**
	tehn • goh keh ah • thehr trahns • bohr • doh
Is this the metro [train] to...?	**¿Es éste el tren a...?**
	ehs ehs • teh ehl trehn ah...

How many stops to…?	**¿Cuántas paradas hay hasta…?**
	kwahn • tahs pah • rah • dahs aye ahs • tah
Where are we?	**¿Dónde estamos?**
	dohn • deh ehs • tah • mohs

For Tickets, see page 43.

BOAT & FERRY

When is the ferry to…?	**¿Cuándo sale el ferry a…?**
	kwahn • doh sah • leh ehl feh • rree ah…
Can I take my car?	**¿Puedo llevar el coche?**
	pweh • doh yeh • bahr ehl koh • cheh
What time is the next sailing?	**¿A qué hora sale el siguiente barco?**
	ah keh oh • rah sah • leh ehl see • geeyehn • teh bahr • koh
Can I book a seat/ cabin?	**¿Puedo reservar un asiento/camarote?**
	pweh • doh reh • sehr • bahr oon ah • seeyehn • toh/kah • mah • roh • teh
How long is the crossing?	**¿Cuánto dura la travesía?**
	kwahn • toh doo • rah lah trah • beh • see • ah

YOU MAY SEE...

BALSA SALVAVIDAS	life boat
CHALECO SALVAVIDAS	life jacket

In Spain, ferry and boat services run to and from the Balearic Islands (Mallorca, Menorca, Ibiza and Formentera), destinations in North Africa and the Canary Islands and ports in Genoa, Italy (from Barcelona) and southern England (from Bilbao and Santander).

TAXI

Where can I get a taxi?	**¿Dónde puedo coger un taxi?** *dohn • deh pweh • doh koh • khehr oon tah • xee*
Can you send a taxi?	**¿Puede enviar un taxi?** *pweh • deh ehn • beeyahr oon tah • xee*
Do you have the number for a taxi?	**¿Tiene el número de alguna empresa de taxi?** *teeyeh • neh ehl noo • meh • roh deh ahl • goo • nah ehm • preh • sah deh tah • xee*
I'd like a taxi now/ for tomorrow at…	**Quiero un taxi ahora/para mañana a la(s)…** *keeyeh • roh oon tah • xee ah • oh • rah/ pah • rah mah • nyah • nah ah lah(s)…*
Pick me up at (place/time)…	**Recójame en/a la(s)…** *reh • koh • khah • meh ehn/ah lah(s)…*
I'm going to…	**Voy…** *boy…*

In Spain, **coger** means to catch or get, as in: **¿Dónde puedo coger un taxi?** (Where can I catch a cab?). However, in Latin America, **coger** is a vulgarity for 'to have sex'. Use **tomar** (**¿Dónde puedo tomar un taxi?**) in Spanish-speaking Latin America.

YOU MAY HEAR…

¿Adónde se dirige? *ah • dohn • deh seh dee • ree • kheh*	Where to?
¿Cuál es la dirección? *kwahl ehs lah dee • rehk • theeyohn*	What's the address?

In major Spanish cities, taxis are reasonably priced. Extra fees are usually charged for trips to the airport, bus station and train station and also for extra luggage. When entering the taxi, make sure the meter is turned on; it should register a base fare when the trip begins. The fare is then increased by a set amount per kilometer traveled.

this address	**a esta dirección**
	ah ehs • tah dee • rehk • theeyohn
the airport	**al aeropuerto**
	ahl ah • eh • roh • pwehr • toh
the train station	**a la estación de trenes**
	ah lah ehs • tah • theeyohn deh treh • nehs
I'm late.	**Llego tarde.**
	yeh • goh tahr • deh
Can you drive faster/slower?	**¿Puede ir más deprisa/despacio?**
	pweh • deh eer mahs deh • pree • sah/ dehs • pah • theeyoh
Stop/Wait here.	**Pare/Espere aquí.**
	pah • reh/ehs • peh • reh ah • kee
How much?	**¿Cuánto es?**
	kwahn • toh ehs
You said it would cost…	**Dijo que costaría…**
	dee • khoh keh kohs • tah • ree • ah…
Keep the change.	**Quédese con el cambio.**
	keh • deh • seh kohn ehl kahm • beeyoh
A receipt, please.	**Un recibo, por favor.**
	oon reh • thee • boh pohr fah • bohr

BICYCLE & MOTORBIKE

I'd like to hire…	**Quiero alquilar…**
	keeyeh • roh ahl • kee • lahr…

a bicycle	**una bicicleta**
	_oo_ • nah bee • thee • _kleh_ • tah
a moped	**un ciclomotor**
	oon thee • kloh • moh • _tohr_
a motorcycle	**una motocicleta**
	_oo_ • nah moh • toh • thee • _kleh_ • tah
How much per day/week?	**¿Cuánto cuesta por día/semana?**
	kwahn • toh _kwehs_ • tah pohr _dee_ • ah/ seh • _mah_ • nah
Can I have a helmet/lock?	**¿Puede darme un casco/candado?**
	pweh • deh _dahr_ • meh oon _kahs_ • koh/ kahn • _dah_ • doh

CAR HIRE

Where's the car hire?	**¿Dónde está el alquiler de coches?**
	dohn • deh ehs • _tah_ ehl ahl • kee • _lehr_ deh _koh_ • chehs
I'd like…	**Quiero…**
	keeyeh • roh…
a cheap/small car	**un coche económico/pequeño**
	oon _koh_ • cheh eh • koh • _noh_ • mee • koh/ peh • _keh_ • nyoh

---

YOU MAY HEAR...

¿Tiene permiso de conducir internacional?
teeyeh • neh pehr • mee • soh deh kohn • doo • theer een • tehr • nah • theeyoh • nahl

Do you have an international driver's license?

Su pasaporte, por favor.
soo pah • sah • pohr • teh pohr fah • bohr

Your passport, please.

¿Quiere seguro?
keeyeh • reh seh • goo • roh

Do you want insurance?

Tiene que dejar una fianza.
teeyeh • neh keh deh • khahr oo • nah fee • ahn • thah

I'll need a deposit.

Firme aquí. *feer • meh ah • kee*

Sign here.

---

an automatic/ a manual	**un coche automático/con transmisión manual**
	oon koh • cheh awtoh • mah • tee • koh/ kohn trahns • mee • seeyohn mah • noo • ahl
air conditioning	**un coche con aire acondicionado**
	oon koh • cheh kohn ayee • reh ah • kohn • dee • theeyoh • nah • doh
a car seat	**un asiento de niño**
	oon ah • seeyehn • toh deh nee • nyoh
How much...?	**¿Cuánto cobran...?**
	kwahn • toh koh • brahn...
per day/week	**por día/semana**
	pohr dee • ah/seh • mah • nah
for...days	**por...días**
	pohr...dee • ahs
per kilometer	**por kilómetro**
	pohr kee • loh • meh • troh
for unlimited mileage	**por kilometraje ilimitado**
	pohr kee • loh • meh • trah • kheh

	ee • lee • mee • <u>tah</u> • doh
with insurance	**con el seguro**
	kohn ehl seh • <u>goo</u> • roh
Are there any discounts?	**¿Ofrecen algún descuento?**
	oh • <u>freh</u> • thehn ahl • <u>goon</u> dehs • <u>kwehn</u> • toh

FUEL STATION

Where's the fuel station?	**¿Dónde está la gasolinera?**
	<u>dohn</u> • deh ehs • <u>tah</u> lah gah • soh • lee • <u>neh</u> • rah
Fill it up.	**Lleno.** <u>yeh</u> • noh
…liters, please.	**…litros, por favor.**
	…<u>lee</u> • trohs pohr fah • <u>bohr</u>
…euros, please.	**Euros por favor.**
	ew-rohs pohr fah-bohr
I'll pay in cash/by credit card.	**Voy a pagar en efectivo/con tarjeta de crédito.**
	boy ah pah • <u>gahr</u> ehn eh • fehk • <u>tee</u> • boh/ kohn tahr • <u>kheh</u> • tah deh <u>kreh</u> • dee • toh

ASKING DIRECTIONS

Is this the way to…?	**¿Es ésta la carretera a…?**
	ehs <u>ehs</u> • tah lah kah • rreh • <u>teh</u> • rah ah…
How far is it to…?	**¿A qué distancia está…?**
	ah keh dees • <u>tahn</u> • theeyah ehs • <u>tah</u>…

YOU MAY SEE…	
NORMAL	regular
SÚPER	super
DIESEL	diesel

YOU MAY HEAR...

todo recto *toh • doh rehk • toh*	straight ahead
a la izquierda *ah lah eeth • keeyehr • dah*	left
a la derecha *ah lah deh • reh • chah*	right
en/doblando la esquina *ehn/doh • blahn • doh lah ehs • kee • nah*	on/around the corner
frente a *frehn • teh ah*	opposite
detrás de *deh • trahs deh*	behind
al lado de *ahl lah • doh deh*	next to
después de *dehs • pwehs deh*	after
al norte/sur *ahl nohr • teh/soor*	north/south
al este/oeste *ahl ehs • teh/oh • ehs • teh*	east/west
en el semáforo *en ehl seh • mah • foh • roh*	at the traffic light
en el cruce *en ehl kroo • theh*	at the intersection

Where's...?	**¿Dónde está...?** *dohn • deh ehs • tah...*
...Street	**la calle...** *lah kah • yeh...*
this address	**ésta dirección** *ehs • tah dee • rek • theeyohn*
the highway [motorway]	**la autopista** *lah aw • toh • pees • tah*

YOU MAY SEE...

	ADELANTAMIENTO PROHIBIDO	no passing zone
STOP	**STOP**	stop
	CALLE DE SENTIDO ÚNICO	one-way street
	CEDA EL PASO	yield [give way]
	ENTRADA PROHIBIDA	no entry
	ESTACIONAMIENTO PROHIBIDO	no parking
	FINAL DEL CARRIL LATERAL DERECHO	right lane ends (merge left)
50	**PROHIBICIÓN VELOCIDAD MÁXIMA**	maximum speed limit

Can you show me on the map?	**¿Me lo puede indicar en el mapa?**	
	meh loh <u>pweh</u> • deh een • dee • <u>kahr</u> ehn ehl <u>mah</u> • pah	
I'm lost.	**Me he perdido.** *meh eh pehr • <u>dee</u> • doh*	

PARKING

Can I park here?	**¿Puedo aparcar aquí?**
	pweh • doh ah • pahr <u>kahr</u> ah • <u>kee</u>
Where's...?	**¿Dónde está**
	<u>dohn</u> • deh ehs • tah

> **i**
>
> When addressing strangers, always use the more
> formal **usted** (singular) or **ustedes** (plural), as opposed to
> the more familiar **tú** (singular) or **vosotros** (plural), until told
> otherwise. If you know someone's title, it's polite to use it,
> e.g., **doctor** (male doctor), **doctora** (female doctor). You can
> also simply say **Señor** (Mr.), **Señora** (Mrs.) or **Señorita** (Miss).

the parking garage/ parking lot?	**el garaje/aparcamiento?**
	ehl gah • rah • kheh/
	ah • pahr • kah • meeyehn • toh
the parking meter?	**el parquímetro?**
	ehl pahr • kee • meh • troh
How much…?	**¿Cuánto cobran…?**
	kwahn • toh koh • brahn…
per hour	**por hora**
	pohr oh • rah
per day	**por día**
	pohr dee • ah
for overnight	**por la noche**
	pohr lah noh • cheh

> **i**
>
> Public parking is noted by a blue sign with a capital 'P'.
> Many towns have **zonas azules** (blue zones), where parking
> is allowed; buy a ticket at the nearby parking machine. Larger
> cities have an **ora zona** (hourly parking). Purchase a ticket
> for 30, 60 or 90 minutes and display it in your windshield.
> Tickets for the **ora zona** can be purchased at tobacconists,
> hotels and other retailers — look for the **ora zona** signs in
> the window. Note: Spain's **Guardia Civil de Tráfico** (highway
> patrol) may enforce payment of fines for illegal parking on the
> spot for non-residents of Spain.

BREAKDOWN & REPAIR

My car broke down/ won't start.	**El coche se me ha averiado/no arranca.** *ehl koh • cheh seh meh ah ah • beh • reeyah • doh/noh ah • rrahn • kah*
Can you fix it (today)?	**¿Puede arreglarlo (hoy mismo)?** *pweh • deh ah • rreh • glahr • loh (oy meez • moh)*
When will it be ready?	**¿Cuándo estará listo?** *kwahn • doh ehs • tah • rah lees • toh*
How much?	**¿Cuánto es?** *kwahn • toh ehs*
I have a puncture/ flat tyre (tire)	**Tengo un neumático pinchado/ desinflado.** *tehn • goh oon neoo • mah • tee • coh peen • chah • doh/dehs • een • flah • doh*

ACCIDENTS

There was an accident.	**Ha habido un accidente.** *ah ah • bee • doh oon ahk • thee • dehn • teh*
Call an ambulance/ the police.	**Llame a una ambulancia/la policía.** *yah • meh ah oo • nah ahm • boo • lahn • theeyah/ lah poh • lee • thee • ah*

PLACES TO STAY

NEED TO KNOW

Can you recommend a hotel?	**¿Puede recomendarme un hotel?** _pweh • deh reh • koh • mehn • <u>dahr</u> • meh oon oh • <u>tehl</u>_
I have a reservation.	**Tengo una reserva.** _<u>tehn</u> • goh <u>oo</u> • nah reh • <u>sehr</u> • bah_
My name is…	**Me llamo…** _meh <u>yah</u> • moh…_
Do you have a room…?	**¿Tienen habitaciones…?** _<u>teeyeh</u> • nehn ah • bee • tah • <u>theeyoh</u> • nehs…_
for one/two	**individuales/dobles** _een • dee • bee • doo • <u>ah</u> • lehs/ <u>doh</u> • blehs_
with a bathroom	**con baño** _kohn <u>bah</u> • nyoh_
with air conditioning	**con aire acondicionado** _kohn <u>ayee</u> • reh ah • kohn • dee • theeyoh • <u>nah</u> • doh_

For...	Para...
	pah • rah...
tonight	**esta noche**
	ehs • tah <u>noh</u> • cheh
two nights	**dos noches**
	dohs <u>noh</u> • chehs
one week	**una semana**
	<u>oo</u> • nah seh • <u>mah</u> • nah
How much?	**¿Cuánto es?**
	<u>kwahn</u> • toh ehs
Is there anything cheaper?	**¿Hay alguna tarifa más barata?**
	aye ahl • <u>goo</u> • nah tah • <u>ree</u> • fah mahs bah • <u>rah</u> • tah
When's check-out?	**¿A qué hora hay que desocupar la habitación?**
	ah keh <u>oh</u> • rah aye keh deh • soh • koo • <u>pahr</u> lah ah • bee • tah • <u>theeyohn</u>
Can I leave this in the safe?	**¿Puedo dejar esto en la caja fuerte?**
	<u>pweh</u> • doh deh • <u>khahr</u> <u>ehs</u> • toh ehn lah <u>kah</u> • khah <u>fwehr</u> • teh
Can I leave my bags?	**¿Podría dejar mi equipaje?**
	poh • <u>dree</u> • ah deh • <u>khahr</u> mee eh • kee • <u>pah</u> • kheh
Can I have the bill/ a receipt?	**¿Me da la factura/un recibo?**
	meh dah lah fahk • <u>too</u> • rah/oon reh • <u>thee</u> • boh
I'll pay in cash/by credit card.	**Voy a pagar en efectivo/con tarjeta de crédito.**
	boy ah pah • <u>gahr</u> ehn eh • fehk • <u>tee</u> • boh/kohn tahr • <u>kheh</u> • tah deh <u>kreh</u> • dee • toh

SOMEWHERE TO STAY

Can you recommend…?	**¿Puede recomendarme…**
	pweh • deh reh • koh • mehn • dahr • meh
a hotel?	**un hotel?**
	oon oh • tehl
a hostel?	**un albergue?**
	oon ahl • behr • geh?
a campsite	**un cámping?**
	oon kahm • peeng?
a bed and breakfast	**una pensión?**
	oo • nah pehn • seeyohn
What is it near?	**¿Qué hay cerca?**
	keh aye thehr • kah
How do I get there?	**¿Cómo se llega allí?**
	koh • moh seh yeh • gah ah • yee

AT THE HOTEL

I have a reservation.	**Tengo una reserva.**
	tehn • goh oo • nah reh • sehr • bah
My name is…	**Me llamo…**
	meh yah • moh…

ⓘ

There's a variety of places to stay in Spain. **Paradores** are government-run inns located throughout the country. These inns are usually castles, monasteries, palaces and other landmark buildings that have been restored and converted into hotels. Reservations are recommended far in advance for **paradores**, as they are very popular, especially in the summer months. Other unique accommodations in Spain include spas, resorts, farm house rentals, apartment rentals, villas and camping.

Do you have a room…?	**¿Tiene una habitación…?** _teeyeh_ • _neh_ <u>oo</u> • _nah_ _ah_ • _bee_ • _tah_ • <u>_theeyohn_</u>…
for one/two	**individual/doble** _een_ • _dee_ • _bee_ • <u>_dwahl_</u> /_doh_ • _bleh_
with a toilet /shower	**con un baño/una ducha** _kohn oon_ <u>_bah_</u> • _nyoh/_<u>oo</u> • _nah doo_ • _chah_
with air conditioning	**con aire acondicionado** _kohn_ <u>_ayee_</u> • _reh_ _ah_ • _kohn_ • _dee_ • _theeyoh_ • <u>_nah_</u> • _doh_
with a single/ double bed	**con una cama/cama de matrimonio** _kohn una_ <u>_kah_</u> • _mah/_<u>_kah_</u> • _mah_ _mah_ • _tree_ • <u>_moh_</u> • _neeyoh_
that's smoking/ non-smoking	**para fumadores/no fumadores** <u>_pah_</u> • _rah foo_ • _mah_ • <u>_doh_</u> • _rehs/_ _noh foo_ • _mah_ • <u>_doh_</u> • _rehs_
For…	**Para…** <u>_pah_</u> • _rah_…
tonight	**esta noche** _ehs_ • _tah noh_ • _cheh_

YOU MAY HEAR…

Su pasaporte/tarjeta de crédito, por favor. _soo pah_ • _sah_ • <u>_pohr_</u> • _teh/tahr_ • <u>_kheh_</u> • _tah deh_ <u>_kreh_</u> • _dee_ • _toh pohr_ _fah_ • <u>_bohr_</u>	Your passport/ credit card, please.
Rellene este formulario. _reh_ • <u>_yeh_</u> • _neh ehs_ • _teh_ _fohr_ • _moo_ • <u>_lah_</u> • _reeyoh_	Fill out this form.
Firme aquí. <u>_feer_</u> • _meh ah_ • <u>_kee_</u>	Sign here.

(i)

When asking for a public restroom, it's more common and polite to use the term **servicio**. The term **baño** tends to be used when asking for a private bathroom such as in a home or a hotel room. Native speakers sometimes use both words interchangeably, but you will almost always see **servicio** on a sign.

(eye icon)

YOU MAY SEE...	
EMPUJAR/TIRAR	push/pull
BAÑO/SERVICIO	bathroom/restroom [toilet]
DUCHA	shower
ASCENSOR	elevator [lift]
ESCALERAS	stairs
LAVANDERÍA	laundry
NO MOLESTAR	do not disturb
PUERTA DE INCENDIOS	fire door
SALIDA (DE EMERGENCIA)	(emergency) exit
LLAMADA DESPERTADOR	wake-up call

two nights	**dos noches**	
	dohs <u>noh</u> • chehs	
a week	**una semana**	
	<u>oo</u> • nah seh • <u>mah</u> • nah	
Does the hotel have...?	**¿Tiene el hotel...?**	
	teeyeh • neh ehl oh • <u>tehl</u>...	
a computer	**un ordenador**	
	oon ohr • deh • nah • <u>dohr</u>	
an elevator [a lift]	**un ascensor**	
	oon ah • thehn • <u>sohr</u>	

(wireless) internet service	**acceso (inalámbrico) a Internet**
	ahk • theh • soh (een • ah • lahm • bree • koh)
	ah een • tehr • neht
room service	**servicio de habitaciones**
	sehr • bee • theeyoh deh
	ah • bee • tah • theeyoh • nehs
a pool	**una piscina**
	oo • nah pees • thee • nah
a gym	**un gimnasio**
	oon kheem • nah • seeyoh
I need…	**Necesito…**
	neh • theh • see • toh…
an extra bed	**otra cama**
	oh • trah kah • mah
a cot	**un catre**
	oon kah • treh
a crib	**una cuna**
	oo • nah koo • nah

For Numbers, see page 20.

PRICE

How much per night/week?	**¿Cuánto cuesta por noche/semana?**
	kwahn • toh kwehs • tah pohr noh • cheh/
	seh • mah • nah
Are there any discounts?	**¿Ofrecen algún descuento?**
	oh • freh • thehn ahl • goon
	dehs • kwehn • toh
Does that include breakfast/sales tax [VAT]?	**¿Incluye el precio el desayuno/IVA?**
	een • kloo • yeh ehl preh • theeyoh
	ehl deh • sah • yoo • noh/eh • beh • ah

PREFERENCES

Can I see the room?	**¿Puedo ver la habitación?**
	pweh • doh behr lah
	ah • bee • tah • _theeyohn_
I'd like a…room.	**Quiero una habitación...**
	keeyeh • roh oo • nah
	ah • bee • tah • theeyohn
better	**mejor**
	meh • khohr
bigger	**más grande**
	mahs grahn • deh
cheaper	**más barata**
	mahs bah • rah • tah
quieter	**más silenciosa**
	mahs see • lehn • _ceeyo_ • sah
I'll take it.	**Me lo llevo**
	meh loh yeh • boh
No, I won't take it.	**No, no me lo llevo**
	noh, noh meh loh yeh • boh

QUESTIONS

Where's…?	**¿Dónde está…?**
	dohn • deh ehs • _tah_…
the bar	**el bar**
	ehl bahr
the bathrooms	**el baño**
	ehl _bah_ • nyoh
the elevator [lift]	**el ascensor**
	ehl ahs • thehn • _sohr_
Can I have…?	**¿Puede darme…?**
	pweh • deh _dahr_ • meh…
a blanket	**una manta**
	_oo_ • nah _mahn_ • tah

an iron	**una plancha**
	_oo_ • nah _plahn_ • chah
a pillow	**una almohada**
	_oo_ • nah ahl • moh • _ah_ • dah
soap	**jabón**
	khah • _bohn_
toilet paper	**papel higiénico**
	pah • _pehl_ ee • _kheeyeh_ • nee • koh
a towel	**una toalla**
	_oo_ • nah toh • _ah_ • yah
Do you have an adapter for this?	**¿Tiene un adaptador para esto?**
	teeyeh • neh oon ah • dahp • tah • _dohr_ pah • rah ehs • toh
How do I turn on the lights?	**¿Cómo enciendo las luces?**
	koh • moh ehn • _theeyehn_ • doh lahs _loo_ • thehs
Can you wake me at…?	**¿Podría despertarme a la/las…?**
	poh • _dree_ • ah dehs • pehr • _tahr_ • meh ah lah/lahs…
Can I leave this in the safe?	**¿Puedo dejar esto en la caja fuerte?**
	pweh • doh deh • _khahr_ ehs • toh ehn lah _kah_ • khah _fwehr_ • teh
Can I have my things from the safe?	**¿Podría darme mis cosas de la caja fuerte?**
	poh • _dree_ • ah _dahr_ • meh mees _koh_ • sahs deh lah _kah_ • khah _fwehr_ • teh
Is there mail [post]/ a message for me?	**¿Hay correo/algún mensaje para mí?**
	aye koh • _rreh_ • oh/ahl • _goon_ mehn • _sah_ • kheh _pah_ • rah mee
Do you have a laundry service?	**¿Tienen servicio de lavandería?**
	teeyeh • nehn sehr • _bee_ • theeyoh deh lah • _bahn_ • deh • _ree_ • ah

For Grammar, see page 12.

PROBLEMS

There's a problem.	**Hay un problema.**
	aye oon proh•bleh•mah
I lost my key/ key card.	**He perdido la llave/llave electrónica.**
	eh pehr•dee•doh lah yah•beh/yah•beh eh•lehk•troh•nee•kah
I've locked my key/ key card in the room.	**He dejado la llave dentro de la habitación.**
	eh deh•khah•doh lah yah•beh dehn•troh deh lah ah•bee•tah•theeyohn
There's no hot water/toilet paper.	**No hay agua caliente/papel higiénico.**
	no aye ah•gwah kah•leeyehn•teh/pah•pehl ee•kheeyeh•nee•koh
The room is dirty.	**La habitación está sucia.**
	lah ah•bee•tah•theeyohn ehs•tah soo•theeyah
There are bugs in the room.	**Hay insectos en la habitación.**
	aye een•sehk•tohs ehn lah ah•bee•tah•theeyohn
…doesn't work.	**…no funciona.**
	… no foon•theeyoh•nah
Can you fix…?	**¿Pueden arreglar…?**
	pweh•dehn ah•rreh•glahr…
the air conditioning	**el aire acondicionado**
	ehl ayee•reh ah•kohn•dee•theeyoh•nah•doh
the fan	**el ventilador**
	ehl behn•tee•lah•dohr

Spain's electricity is 220 volts. You may need a converter and/or an adapter for your appliances.

the heat [heating]	**la calefacción**
	lah kah • leh • fahk • theeyohn
the light	**la luz** *lah looth*
the TV	**la televisión**
	lah teh • leh • bee • seeyohn
the toilet	**el retrete**
	ehl reh • treh • teh
I'd like another room.	**Quiero otra habitación.**
	keeyeh • roh oh • trah ah • bee • tah • theeyohn

CHECKING OUT

When's check-out?	**¿A qué hora hay que desocupar la habitación?** *ah keh oh • rah aye keh deh • soh • koo • pahr lah ah • bee • tah • theeyohn*
Can I leave my bags here until…?	**¿Puedo dejar mi equipaje aquí hasta…?** *pweh • doh deh • khahr mee eh • kee • pah • kheh ah • kee ahs • tah…*
Can I have an itemized bill/a receipt?	**¿Puede darme una factura detallada/un recibo?** *pweh • deh dahr • meh oo • nah fahk • too • rah deh • tah • yah • dah/ oon reh • thee • boh*

I think there's a mistake.	**Creo que hay un error.**
	kreh • oh keh aye oon eh • rrohr
I made… phone calls.	**He hecho…llamadas.**
	eh eh • choh… yah • mah • dahs
I took…from the mini-bar.	**He tomado…del minibar.**
	eh toh • mah • doh… dehl mee • nee • bar
I'll pay in cash/ by credit card.	**Voy a pagar en efectivo/con tarjeta de crédito.**
	boy ah pah • gahr ehn eh • fehk • tee • boh/ kohn tahr • kheh • tah deh kreh • dee • toh

RENTING

I reserved an apartment/a room.	**He reservado un apartamento/ una habitación.**
	eh reh • sehr • bah • doh oon ah • pahr • tah • mehn • toh/ oo • nah ah • bee • tah • theeyohn
My name is…	**Me llamo…**
	meh yah • moh…
Can I have the key/key card?	**¿Puede darme la llave/llave electrónica?**
	pweh • deh dahr • meh lah yah • beh/ yah • beh eh • lehk • troh • nee • kah
Are there…?	**¿Hay…?**
	aye…
dishes	**platos**
	plah • tohs
pillows	**almohadas**
	ahl • moh • ah • dahs
sheets	**sábanas**
	sah • bah • nahs
towels	**toallas**
	toh • ah • yahs
kitchen utensils	**cubiertos**
	koo • beeyehr • tohs

When do I put out the bins/ recycling?	**¿Cuándo saco la basura/el reciclado?**
	kwahn • doh sah • koh lah bah • soo • rah/ ehl reh • thee • klah • doh
…is broken.	**…está estropeado** *m/***estropeada** *f.*
	…ehs • tah ehs • troh • peh • ah • doh/ ehs • troh • peh • ah • dah
How does… work?	**¿Cómo funciona…?**
	koh • moh foon • theeyoh
the air conditioner	**el aire acondicionado**
	ehl ayee • reh ah • kohn • dee • theeyoh • nah • doh
the dishwasher	**el lavavajillas**
	ehl lah • bah • bah • khee • yahs
the freezer	**el congelador**
	ehl kohn • kheh • lah • dohr
the heater	**la calefacción**
	lah kah • leh • fahk • theeyohn
the microwave	**el microondas**
	ehl mee • kroh • ohn • dahs
the refrigerator	**la nevera**
	lah neh • beh • rah
the stove	**el horno**
	ehl ohr • noh
the washing machine	**la lavadora**
	lah lah • bah • doh • rah

DOMESTIC ITEMS

I need…	**Necesito…** *neh • theh • see • toh…*
an adapter	**un adaptador**
	oon ah • dahp • tah • dohr
aluminum [kitchen] foil	**papel de aluminio**
	pah • pehl deh ah • loo • mee • neeyoh
a bottle opener	**un abrebotellas**
	oon ah • breh • boh • teh • yahs

a broom	**una escoba**
	oo • nah ehs • koh • bah
a can opener	**un abrelatas**
	oon ah • breh • lah • tahs
cleaning supplies	**productos de limpieza**
	proh • dook • tohs
	deh leem • peeyeh • thah
a corkscrew	**un sacacorchos**
	oon sah • kah • kohr • chohs
detergent	**detergente**
	deh • tehr • khehn • teh
dishwashing liquid	**líquido lavavajillas**
	lee • kee • doh lah • bah • bah • khee • yahs
bin bags	**bolsas de basura**
	bohl • sahs deh bah • soo • rah
a lightbulb	**una bombilla**
	oo • nah bohm • bee • yah
matches	**cerillas**
	theh • ree • yahs
a mop	**una fregona**
	oo • nah freh • goh • nah
napkins	**servilletas**
	sehr • bee • yeh • tahs
paper towels	**papel de cocina**
	pah • pehl deh koh • thee • nah
plastic wrap [cling film]	**film transparente**
	feelm trahns • pah • rehn • teh
a plunger	**un desatascador**
	oon deh • sah • tahs • kah • dohr
scissors	**tijeras**
	tee • kheh • rahs
a vacuum cleaner	**una aspiradora**
	oo • nah ahs • pee • rah • doh • rah

For In the Kitchen, see page 190.

AT THE HOSTEL

Is there a bed available?	**¿Hay camas disponibles?**
	aye kah • mahs dees • poh • nee • blehs
I'd like…	**¿Me puede dar…?**
	meh pweh • deh dahr…
a single/ double room	**una habitación individual/doble**
	oo • nah ah • bee • tah • theeyohn
	een • dee • bee • doo • ahl/doh • bleh
a blanket	**una manta**
	oo • nah mahn • tah
a pillow	**una almohada**
	oo • nah ahl • moh • ah • dah
sheets	**sábanas**
	sah • bah • nahs
a towel	**una toalla**
	oo • nah toh • ah • yah

> (i)
>
> With more than 100 hostels around Spain, finding an inexpensive place to stay should be easy. Hostels are inexpensive accommodations that have dormitory-style rooms and, sometimes, private or semi-private rooms. Some offer private bathrooms, though most have shared facilities. There is usually a self-service kitchen on site. Reservations are recommended in advance in larger cities and popular destinations during the tourist season.

Do you have lockers?	**¿Tienen consignas?**
	teeyeh • nehn kohn • seeg • nahs
When do you lock up?	**¿A qué hora cierran las puertas?**
	ah keh oh • rah theeyeh • rrahn lahs
	pwehr • tahs

Do I need a membership card?	**¿Necesito una tarjeta de socio?**
	neh • theh • <u>see</u> • toh <u>oo</u> • nah tahr • <u>kheh</u> • tah de soh • theeyoh
Here's my International Student Card.	**Aquí tiene mi carnet internacional de estudiante.**
	ah • <u>kee</u> teeyeh • neh mee kahr • <u>neht</u> een • tehr • nah • theeyoh • <u>nahl</u> deh ehs • too • <u>deeyahn</u> • teh

GOING CAMPING

Can I camp here?	**¿Puedo acampar aquí?**
	<u>pweh</u> • doh ah • kahm • <u>pahr</u> ah • kee
Where's the campsite?	**¿Dónde está el cámping?**
	<u>dohn</u> • deh ehs • <u>tah</u> ehl <u>kahm</u> • peeng
What is the charge per day/week?	**¿Cuánto cobran por día/semana?**
	<u>kwahn</u> • toh <u>koh</u> • brahn pohr <u>dee</u> • ah/ seh • <u>mah</u> • nah
Are there…?	**¿Hay…?**
	aye…
cooking facilities	**instalaciones para cocinar**
	eens • tah • lah • <u>theeyoh</u> • nehs pah • rah koh • thee • <u>nahr</u>
electric outlets	**enchufes eléctricos**
	ehn • <u>choo</u> • fehs eh • <u>lehk</u> • tree • kohs
laundry facilities	**servicio de lavandería**
	sehr • <u>bee</u> • theeyoh deh lah • bahn • deh • <u>ree</u> • ah

---

YOU MAY SEE…

AGUA POTABLE	drinking water
PROHIBIDO ACAMPAR	no camping
PROHIBIDO HACER HOGUERAS/	no fires/
BARBACOAS	barbecues

showers	**duchas**
	doo • chahs
tents for hire	**tiendas de alquiler**
	teeyehn • dahs deh ahl • kee • _lehr_
Where can I empty the chemical toilet?	**¿Dónde puedo vaciar el váter químico?**
	dohn • deh _pweh_ • doh bah • thee • _ahr_ ehl
	bah • tehr _kee_ • mee • koh

For Domestic Items, see page 77.

COMMUNICATIONS

NEED TO KNOW

Where's an internet cafe?	**¿Dónde hay un cibercafé?**
	dohn • deh aye oon
	thee • _behr_ • kah • _feh_
Can I access the internet/check e-mail?	**¿Puedo acceder a Internet/revisar el correo electrónico?**
	pweh • doh ahk • theh • _dehr_
	ah een • tehr • _neht_/reh • bee • _sahr_
	ehl koh • _rreh_ • oh
	eh • lehk • _troh_ • nee • koh
How much per (half) hour?	**¿Cuánto cuesta por (media) hora?**
	kwahn • toh _kwehs_ • tah pohr
	(_meh_) • deeyah) _oh_ • rah
How do I connect/ log on?	**¿Cómo entro al sistema/inicio la sesión?**
	koh • moh _ehn_ • troh ahl
	sees • _teh_ • mah/ee • nee • _theeyoh_ lah
	seh • _seeyohn_

A phone card, please.	**Una tarjeta telefónica, por favor.** _oo_ • nah tahr • _kheh_ • tah teh • _leh_ • _foh_ • nee • kah pohr fah • _bohr_
Can I have your phone number?	**¿Me puede dar su número de teléfono?** meh _pweh_ • deh dahr soo _noo_ • meh • roh deh teh • _leh_ • foh • noh
Here's my number/ e-mail address.	**Aquí tiene mi número/ dirección de correo electrónico.** ah • _kee teeyeh_ • neh mee _noo_ • meh • roh/dee • rehk • _theeyohn_ deh koh • _rreh_ • oh eh • lehk • _troh_ • nee • koh
Call me.	**Llámeme.** _yah_ • meh • meh
E-mail me.	**Envíeme un correo.** ehn • _bee_ • eh • meh oon koh • _rreh_ • oh
Hello. This is…	**Hola. Soy…** _oh_ • lah soy…
Can I speak to…?	**¿Puedo hablar con…?** _pweh_ • doh ah • _blahr_ kohn…
Can you repeat that?	**¿Puede repetir eso?** _pweh_ • deh reh • peh • _teer eh_ • soh
I'll call back later.	**Llamaré más tarde.** yah • mah • _reh_ mahs tahr • deh
Bye.	**Adiós.** ah • _deeyohs_
Where's the post office?	**¿Dónde está la oficina de correos?** _dohn_ • deh ehs • _tah_ lah oh • fee • _thee_ • nah deh koh • _rreh_ • ohs
I'd like to send this to…	**Quiero mandar esto a…** _keeyeh_ • roh mahn • _dahr ehs_ • toh ah…

ONLINE

Where's an internet cafe?	**¿Dónde hay un cibercafé?** *dohn • deh aye oon thee • behr • kah • feh*
Does it have wireless internet?	**¿Tiene Internet inalámbrico?** *teeyeh • neh een • tehr • neht een • ah • lahm • bree • koh*
What is the WiFi password?	**¿Cuál es la contraseña de WiFI?** *kwahl ehs lah kohn • trah • seh • nyah deh weeh • feeh*
Is the WiFi free?	**¿Es gratuito el acceso WiFi?** *esh grah • too • ee • toh ehl ahk • theh • soh weeh • feeh*
Do you have bluetooth?	**¿Tiene Bluetooth?** *teeyeh • neh blue • tooth*
How do I turn the computer on/off?	**¿Cómo enciendo/apago el ordenador?** *koh • moh ehn • theeyen • doh/ ah • pah • goh ehl ohr • deh • nah • dohr*
Can I…?	**¿Puedo…?** *pweh • doh…*
access the internet	**acceder a Internet** *ahk • theh • dehr ah een • tehr • neht*
check e-mail	**revisar el correo electrónico** *reh • bee • sahr ehl koh • rreh • oh eh • lehk • troh • nee • koh*
print	**imprimir** *eem • pree • meer*
plug in/charge my laptop/iPhone/ iPad/BlackBerry?	**enchufar/cargar el portátil/iPhone/ iPad/Blackberry?** *ehn • choo • fahr/kahr • gahr ehl pohr • tah • teel/i fon/i pad/Blackberry*
access Skype?	**acceder a Skype?** *ahk • theh • dehr ah skype*

How much per (half) hour?	**¿Cuánto cuesta por (media) hora?**
	kwahn • toh kwehs • tah pohr (meh • deeyah)
	oh • rah
How do I...?	**¿Cómo...?**
	koh • moh...
connect/	**me conecto/me desconecto**
disconnect	_meh koh • nehk • toh/meh dehs • koh •_
	nehk • toh
log on/off	**inicio/cierro la sesión**
	ee • nee • theeyoh/theeyeh • rroh
	lah seh • seeyohn
type this symbol	**escribo este símbolo**
	ehs • kree • boh ehs • teh seem • boh • loh
What's your e-mail?	**¿Cuál es su dirección de correo electrónico?**
	kwahl ehs soo dee • rehk • theeyohn
	deh koh • rreh • oh eh • lehk •
	troh • nee • koh
My e-mail is...	**Mi dirección de correo electrónico es...**
	mee dee • rehk • theeyohn deh koh • rreh •
	oh eh • lehk • troh • nee • koh ehs...
Do you have a scanner?	**¿Tienen un escáner?**
	teeyeh • nehn oon ehs • kah • nehr

SOCIAL MEDIA

Are you on Twitter?	**¿Está en Facebook/Twitter?**
	(polite form) ehs • tah ehn
	Facebook/Twitter
	¿Estás en Facebook/Twitter?
	(informal form)
	ehs • tahs ehn Facebook/Twitter
What's your user name?	**¿Cuál es su nombre de usuario?**
	(polite form) kwahl ehs soo nohm • breh
	deh oo • soo • ah • reeyoh

YOU MAY SEE...

CERRAR	close
BORRAR	delete
CORREO ELECTRÓNICO	e-mail
SALIR	exit
AYUDA	help
MENSAJERO INSTANTÁNEO	instant messenger
INTERNET	internet
INICIO DE SESIÓN	login
NUEVO (MENSAJE)	new (message)
ENCENDER/APAGAR	on/off
ABRIR	open
IMPRIMIR	print
GUARDAR	save
ENVIAR	send
NOMBRE DE USUARIO/CONTRASEÑA	username/password
INTERNET INALÁMBRICO	wireless internet

¿Cuál es tu nombre de usuario?
(informal form) kwahl ehs too nohm • breh deh oo • soo • ah • reeyoh

I'll add you as a friend.
Le añadiré como amigo.
(polite form) leh ah • nyah • dee • reh koh • moh ah • mee • goh

Te añadiré como amigo.
(informal form) teh ah • nyah • dee • reh koh • moh ah • mee • goh

I'll follow you on Twitter.
Le seguiré en Twitter.
(polite form) leh seh • gee • reh ehn Twitter

Te seguiré en Twitter.
(informal form) teh seh • gee • reh ehn Twitter

Are you following...?	**¿Sigue a...?** *(polite form) see • geh ah* **¿Sigues a...?** *(informal form) see • gehs ah*
I'll put the pictures on Facebook/Twitter.	**Subiré las fotos a Facebook/Twitter.** *soo • bee • reh lahs foh • tohs ah Facebook/ Twitter*
I'll tag you in the pictures.	**Le etiquetaré en las fotos.** *(polite form) leh eh • tee • keh • tah • reh ehn lahs foh • tohs* **Te etiquetaré en las fotos.** *(informal form)* *teh eh • tee • keh • tah • reh ehn lahs foh • tohs*

PHONE

A phone card/ prepaid phone, please.	**Una tarjeta telefónica/Un teléfono prepago, por favor.** *oo • nah tahr • kheh • tah teh • leh • foh • nee • kah/oon teh • leh • foh • noh preh • pah • goh pohr fah • bohr*
How much?	**¿Cuánto es?** *kwahn • toh ehs*
Where's the pay phone?	**¿Dónde está el teléfono público?** *dohn • deh ehs • tah ehl teh • leh • foh • noh poo • blee • koh*
What's the area code/ country code for...?	**¿Cuál es el prefijo/código de país para...?** *kwahl ehs ehl preh • fee • khoh/ koh • dee • goh deh pah • ees pah • rah...*
What's the number for Information?	**¿Cuál es el número de información?** *kwahl ehs ehl noo • meh • roh deh een • fohr • mah • theeyohn*
I'd like the number for...	**Quiero que me dé el número de teléfono de...** *keeyeh • roh keh meh deh ehl noo • meh • roh deh teh • leh • foh • noh deh...*

I'd like to call collect [reverse the charges].	**Quiero llamar a cobro revertido** *keeyeh • roh yah • mahr ah koh • broh reh • behr • tee • doh*
My phone doesn't work here.	**Mi teléfono no funciona aquí.** *mee teh • <u>leh</u> • foh • noh no foon • <u>theeyoh</u> • nah ah • <u>kee</u>*
What network are you on?	**¿En qué red está?** *ehn keh rehd ehs • tah*
Is it 3G?	**¿Es 3G?** *ehs trehs kheh*
I have run out of credit/minutes.	**Me he quedado sin saldo/minutos.** *meh eh keh • dah • doh seen sahl • doh/ meeh • noo • tohs*
Can I buy some credit?	**¿Puedo comprar una recarga de saldo?** *pweh • doh kohm • prahr oo • nah reh • kahr • gah deh sahl • doh*
Do you have a phone charger?	**¿Tiene un cargador de móvil?** *teeyeh • neh oon kahr • gah • dohr deh moh • beel*
Can I have your number?	**¿Me puede dar su número de teléfono?** *meh <u>pweh</u> • deh dahr soo <u>noo</u> • meh • roh deh teh • <u>leh</u> • foh • noh*
Here's my number.	**Aquí tiene mi número.** *ah • <u>kee</u> <u>teeyeh</u> • neh mee <u>noo</u> • meh • roh*

Please call me.	**Llámame, por favor.**
	yah • mah • meh pohr fah • _bohr_
Please text me.	**Envíame un mensaje de texto, por favor.**
	ehn • _beeyah_ • meh oon mehn • _sah_ • kheh
	deh _tehx_ • toh pohr fah • _bohr_
I'll call you.	**Le m /La f llamaré.**
	leh/lah yah • mah • _reh_
I'll text you.	**Te enviaré un mensaje de texto.**
	teh ehn • beeyah • _reh_ oon
	mehn • _sah_ • kheh deh _tehx_ • toh

TELEPHONE ETIQUETTE

Hello. This is…	**Hola. Soy…**
	_oh_ • lah soy…
Can I speak to…?	**¿Puedo hablar con…?**
	pweh • doh ah • _blahr_ kohn…
Extension…	**Extensión…**
	ehks • tehn • _seeyohn_…
Speak louder/more slowly, please.	**Hable más alto/despacio, por favor.**
	_ah_ • bleh mahs _ahl_ • toh/dehs • _pah_ •
	theeyoh pohr fah • _bohr_
Can you repeat that?	**¿Puede repetir eso?**
	pweh • deh reh • peh • _teer eh_ • soh
I'll call back later.	**Llamaré más tarde.**
	yah • mah • _reh_ mahs _tahr_ • deh
Bye.	**Adiós.**
	ah • _deeyohs_

When someone answers the telephone in Spain, you will hear them say **Dígame** - literally "Tell me". This is the caller's cue to go ahead and introduce themselves and state who you want to speak to.

FAX

Can I send/receive a fax here?	**¿Puedo enviar/recibir un fax aquí?** *pweh • doh ehn • bee • ahr/reh • thee • beer oon fahx ah • kee*
What's the fax number?	**¿Cuál es el número de fax?** *kwahl ehs ehl noo • meh • roh deh fahx*
Please fax this to…	**Por favor envíe este fax a…** *pohr fah • bohr ehn • bee • eh ehs • teh fahx ah…*

YOU MAY HEAR…

¿Quién llama? *keeyehn yah • mah*	Who's calling?
Espere. *ehs • peh • reh*	Hold on.
Le paso. *leh pah • soh*	I'll put you through.
No está. *noh ehs • tah*	He/She is not here.
No puede atenderle en este momento. *noh pweh • deh ah • tehn • dehr • leh ehn ehs • teh moh • mehn • toh*	He/She can't come to the phone.
¿Quiere dejarle un mensaje? *keeyeh • reh deh • khahr • leh oon mehn • sah • kheh*	Would you like to leave a message?
Vuelva a llamar más tarde/en diez minutos. *bwehl • bah ah yah • mahr mahs tahr • deh/ehn deeyeth mee • noo • tohs*	Call back later/ in 10 minutes.
¿Le puede llamar él m/ella f a usted? *leh pweh • deh yah • mahr ehl/eh • yah ah oos • tehth*	Can he/she call you back?
¿Me da su número? *meh dah soo noo • meh • roh*	What's your number?

POST

Where's the post office/mailbox?	**¿Dónde está la oficina/el buzón de correos?** _dohn_ • deh ehs • _tah_ lah oh • fee • _thee_ • nah/ ehl boo • _thohn_ deh koh • _rreh_ • ohs
A stamp for this postcard/letter to…	**Un sello para esta postal/carta a…** oon _seh_ • yoh _pah_ • rah ehs • tah pohs • _tahl_/ _kahr_ • tah ah…
How much?	**¿Cuánto es?** _kwahn_ • toh ehs
I want to send this package by airmail/express.	**Quiero mandar este paquete por correo aéreo/urgente.** _keeyeh_ • roh mahn • _dahr ehs_ • teh pah • _keh_ • teh pohr koh • _rreh_ • oh ah • _eh_ • reh • oh/oor • _khen_ • teh
A receipt, please.	**Un recibo, por favor.** oon reh • _thee_ • boh pohr fah • _bohr_

YOU MAY HEAR…

Rellene la declaración para la aduana.
reh • _yeh_ • neh lah deh • klah • rah •
theeyohn pah • rah lah ah • doo • _ah_ • nah

¿Qué valor tiene?
keh bah • _lohr teeyeh_ • neh

¿Qué hay dentro?
keh aye _dehn_ • troh

Fill out the customs declaration form.

What's the value?

What's inside?

Oficinas de Correos (post offices) in Spain offer more than just standard postal services. You may be able to do banking, scan and e-mail documents and send money orders from the local post office. Services available vary by location.

SIGHTSEEING

ESSENTIAL

Where's the tourist information office?	**¿Dónde está la oficina de turismo?** _dohn • deh ehs • tah lah oh • fee • thee • nah deh too • rees • moh_
What are the main sights?	**¿Dónde están los principales sitios de interés?** _dohn • deh ehs • tahn lohs preen • thee • pah • lehs see • teeyohs deh een • teh • rehs_
Do you have tours in English?	**¿Hay visitas en inglés?** _aye bee • see • tahs ehn een • glehs_
Can I have a map/guide?	**¿Puede darme un mapa/una guía?** _pweh • deh dahr • meh oon mah • pah/ oo • nah gee • ah_

TOURIST INFORMATION

Do you have information on…?	**¿Tiene información sobre…?** _teeyeh • neh een • fohr • mah • theeyohn soh • breh…_

ⓘ

Tourist offices are located in major Spanish cities and in many of the smaller towns that are popular tourist attractions. Ask at your hotel or check online to find the nearest office.

Can you recommend…?	**¿Puede recomendarme…?**
	pweh • deh reh • koh • mehn • dahr • meh…
a bus tour	**un recorrido en autobús**
	oon reh • koh • rree • doh ehn awtoh • boos
an excursion to…	**una excursión a…**
	oo • nah ehx • koor • seeyohn ah…
a sightseeing tour	**un recorrido turístico**
	oon reh • koh • rree • doh
	too • rees • tee • koh

ON TOUR

I'd like to go on the tour to…	**Quiero ir a la visita de…**
	keeyeh • roh eer ah lah bee • see • tah deh…
When's the next tour?	**¿Cuándo es la próxima visita?**
	kwahn • doh ehs lah proh • xee • mah
	bee • see • tah
Are there tours in English?	**¿Hay visitas en inglés?**
	aye bee • see • tahs ehn een • glehs
Is there an English guide book/audio guide?	**¿Hay una guía/audioguía en inglés?**
	aye oo • nah gee • ah/
	awoo • deeyoh • gee • ah ehn een • glehs
What time do we leave/return?	**¿A qué hora salimos/volvemos?**
	ah keh oh • rah sah • lee • mohs/
	bohl • beh • mohs
We'd like to see…	**Queremos ver…**
	keh • reh • mohs behr…

Can we stop here...?	**¿Podemos parar aquí...?**
	poh • deh • mohs pah • rahr ah • kee...
to take photos	**para tomar fotos**
	pah • rah toh • mahr foh • tohs
for souvenirs	**para comprar recuerdos**
	pah • rah kohm • prahr reh • kwehr • dohs
for the toilet	**para ir al servicio**
	pah • rah eer ahl sehr • bee • theeyoh
Is it disabled-accessible?	**¿Tiene acceso para discapacitados?**
	teeyeh • neh ahk • theh • soh pah • rah
	dees • kah • pah • thee • tah • dohs

SEEING THE SIGHTS

Where is/are...?	**¿Dónde está/están...?**
	dohn • deh ehs • tah/ehs • tahn...
the battleground	**el campo de batalla**
	ehl kahm • poh deh bah • tah • yah
the botanical garden	**el jardín botánico**
	ehl khahr • deen boh • tah • nee • koh
the castle	**el castillo**
	ehl kahs • tee • yoh
the downtown area	**el centro**
	ehl thehn • troh
the fountain	**la fuente**
	lah fwehn • teh
the library	**la biblioteca**
	lah bee • bleeyoh • teh • kah
the market	**el mercado**
	ehl mehr • kah • doh
the museum	**el museo**
	ehl moo • seh • oh
the old town	**el casco antiguo**
	ehl kahs • koh ahn •
	tee • gwoh

the opera house	**teatro de la ópera**
	ehl tehahtroh deh lah operh rah
the palace	**el palacio**
	ehl pah • lah • theeyoh
the park	**el parque**
	ehl pahr • keh
the ruins	**las ruinas**
	lahs rwee • nahs
the shopping area	**la zona comercial**
	lahs thoh • nah koh • mehr • theeyahl
the town square	**la plaza**
	lah plah • thah
Can you show me on the map?	**¿Puede indicármelo en el mapa?**
	pweh • deh een • dee • kahr • meh • loh
	ehn ehl mah • pah
It's…	**Es…**
	ehs…
amazing	**increíble**
	een • kreh • ee • bleh
beautiful	**precioso**
	preh • theeyoh • soh
boring	**aburrido**
	ah • boo • rree • don

interesting	**interesante**
	een • teh • reh • <u>sahn</u> • teh
magnificent	**magnífico**
	mahg • <u>nee</u> • fee • koh
romantic	**romántico**
	roh • <u>mahn</u> • tee • koh
strange	**extraño**
	ex • <u>trah</u> • nyon
stunning	**impresionante**
	eem • preh • seeyoh • <u>nahn</u> • teh
terrible	**horrible**
	oh • <u>rree</u> • bleh
ugly	**feo**
	<u>feh</u> • oh
I (don't) like it.	**(No) Me gusta.**
	(noh) meh <u>goo</u> • stah

RELIGIOUS SITES

Where is…?	**¿Dónde está…?**
	<u>dohn</u> • deh ehs • <u>tah</u>…
the cathedral	**la catedral**
	lah kah • teh • <u>drahl</u>

the Catholic/ Protestant church	**la iglesia católica/protestante** *lah ee • gleh • seeyah kah • toh • lee • kah/* *proh • tehs • tahn • teh*
the mosque	**la mezquita** *lah mehth • kee • tah*
the shrine	**el santuario** *ehl sahn • twah • reeyoh*
the synagogue	**la sinagoga** *lah see • nah • goh • gah*
the temple	**el templo** *ehl tehm • ploh*
What time is mass/the service?	**¿A qué hora es la misa/el culto?** *ah keh oh • rah ehs lah mee • sah/* *ehl kool • toh*

ACTIVITIES

SHOPPING

NEED TO KNOW

Where's the market/ mall?
¿Dónde está el mercado/ centro comercial?

dohn • deh ehs • _tah_ ehl mehr • _kah_ • doh/ _then_ • troh koh • mehr • _theeyahl_

I'm just looking.
Sólo estoy mirando.
soh • loh ehs • _toy_ mee • _rahn_ • doh

Can you help me?
¿Puede ayudarme?
pweh • deh ah • yoo • _dahr_ • meh

I'm being helped.
Ya me atienden.
yah meh ah • _teeyehn_ • dehn

How much?
¿Cuánto es?
kwahn • toh ehs

That one, please.
Ése _m_/**Ésa** _f_, **por favor.**
eh • she/_eh_ • sah pohr fah • _bohr_

That's all.
Eso es todo.
_eh_ • soh ehs toh • doh

Where can I pay?
¿Dónde se paga?
dohn • deh seh _pah_ • gah

I'll pay in cash/by credit card.	**Voy a pagar en efectivo/ con tarjeta de crédito.**
	boy ah pah • gahr ehn eh • fehk • tee • boh/kohn tahr • kheh • tah deh kreh • dee • toh
A receipt, please.	**Un recibo, por favor.**
	oon reh • thee • boh pohr fah • bohr

AT THE SHOPS

Where is/are…?	**¿Dónde está/están…?**
	dohn • deh ehs • tah/ehs • tahn…
the antiques store	**la tienda de antigüedades**
	lah teeyehn • dah deh ahn • tee • gweh • dah • dehs
the bakery	**la panadería**
	lah pah • nah • deh • ree • ah
the bank	**el banco**
	ehl bahn • koh
the bookstore	**la librería**
	lah lee • breh • ree • ah
the clothing store	**la tienda de ropa**
	lah teeyehn • dah deh roh • pah
the delicatessen	**la charcutería**
	lah chahr • koo • teh • ree • ah
the department stores	**los grandes almacenes**
	lohs grahn • dehs ahl • mah • theh • nehs

Spanish markets can be great for fruit and vegetables, antiques, souvenirs and regional specialty items. Your hotel or local tourist office will have information on the markets in your area. Most permanent markets are open daily from early morning until early afternoon.

the gift shop	**la tienda de regalos**
	lah teeyehn • dah deh reh • gah • lohs
the health food store	**la tienda de alimentos naturales**
	lah teeyehn • dah deh ah • lee • mehn •
	tohs nah • too • rahl • ehs
the jeweler	**la joyería**
	lah khoh • yeh • ree • ah
the liquor store [off-licence]	**la tienda de bebidas alcohólicas**
	lah teeyehn • dah deh beh • bee • dahs
	ahl • koh • oh • lee • kahs
the market	**el mercado**
	ehl mehr • kah • doh
the music store	**la tienda de música**
	lah teeyehn • dah deh moo • see • kah
the pastry shop	**la pastelería**
	lah pahs • teh • leh • ree • ah
the pharmacy [chemist]	**la farmacia**
	lah fahr • mah • theeyah
the produce [grocery] store	**la tienda de frutas y verduras**
	lah teeyehn • dah deh froo • tahs ee
	behr • doo • rahs
the shoe store	**la zapatería**
	lah thah • pah • teh • ree • ah
the shopping mall	**el centro comercial**
	ehl then • troh koh • mehr • theeyahl
the souvenir store	**la tienda de recuerdos**
	lah teeyehn • dah deh reh • kwehr • dohs
the supermarket	**el supermercado**
	ehl soo • pehr • mehr • kah • doh
the tobacconist	**el estanco**
	ehl ehs • tahn • koh
the toy store	**la juguetería**
	lah khoo • geh • teh • ree • ah

YOU MAY SEE...

ABIERTO/CERRADO	open/closed
CERRADO AL MEDIODIA	closed for lunch
PROBADOR	fitting room
CAJERO *m* **CAJERA** *f*	cashier
SOLO EFECTIVO	cash only
SE ACEPTAN TARJETAS DE CREDITO	credit cards accepted
HORARIO DE APERTURA	business hours
SALIDA	exit

ASK AN ASSISTANT

When do you open/close?	**¿A qué hora abren/cierran?** *ah keh oh • rah ah • brehn/theeyeh • rrahn*
Where is/are...?	**¿Dónde está/están...?** *dohn • deh ehs • tah/ehs • tahn...*
the cashier	**la caja** *lah kah • khah*
the escalators	**las escaleras mecánicas** *lahs ehs • kah • leh • rahs meh • kah • nee • kahs*

YOU MAY HEAR...

¿Necesita ayuda? *neh • theh • see • tah ah • yoo • dah*	Can I help you?
Un momento. *oon moh • mehn • toh*	One moment.
¿Qué desea? *keh deh • seh • ah*	What would you like?
¿Algo más? *ahl • goh mahs*	Anything else?

the elevator [lift]	**el ascensor**
	ehl ahs • thehn • sohr
the fitting room	**el probador**
	ehl proh • bah • dohr
the store directory	**la guía de tiendas**
	lah gee • ah deh teeyehn • dahs
Can you help me?	**¿Puede ayudarme?**
	pweh • deh ah • yoo • dahr • meh
I'm just looking.	**Sólo estoy mirando.**
	soh • loh ehs • toy mee • rahn • doh
I'm being helped.	**Ya me atienden.**
	yah meh ah • teeyehn • dehn
Do you have…?	**¿Tienen…?**
	teeyeh • nehn…
Can you show me…?	**¿Podría enseñarme…?**
	poh • dree • ah ehn • seh • nyahr • meh…
Can you ship/ wrap it?	**¿Pueden hacer un envío/envolverlo?**
	pweh • dehn ah • thehr oon ehn • bee • oh/ ehn • bohl • behr • loh
How much?	**¿Cuánto es?**
	kwahn • toh ehs
That's all.	**Eso es todo.**
	eh • soh ehs toh • doh

For Clothes & Accessories, see page 113.

PERSONAL PREFERENCES

I'd like something…	**Quiero algo…**
	keeyeh • roh ahl • goh…
cheap/expensive	**barato/caro**
	bah • rah • toh/kah • roh
larger/smaller	**más grande/más pequeño**
	mahs grahn • deh/mahs peh • keh • nyoh
from this region	**de esta región**
	deh ehs • tah reh • kheeyohn

Credit cards are widely accepted throughout Spain; be prepared though, you may be asked to show ID when using a credit card. Mastercard™ and Visa™ are the most commonly used; American Express® is accepted in most places.
Debit cards are common in Spain and throughout Europe; these are usually accepted if backed by Visa™ or Mastercard™. Traveler's checks are not accepted everywhere. Smaller stores and stands such as newsstands, tobacconists, flower shops and markets will take cash only.

YOU MAY HEAR...

¿Cómo va a pagar?
koh • moh bah ah pah • gahr

How are you paying?

Su tarjeta ha sido rechazada.
soo tahr • kheh • tah ah see • doh reh • chah • thah • dah

Your credit card has been declined.

Su documento de identidad, por favor.
soo doh • koo • mehn • toh deh ee • dehn • tee • dahd pohr fah • bohr

ID, please.

No aceptamos tarjetas de crédito.
noh ah • thehp • tah • mohs tahr • kheh • tahs deh kreh • dee • toh

We don't accept credit cards.

Sólo en efectivo, por favor.
soh • loh ehn eh • fehk • tee • boh pohr fah • bohr

Cash only, please.

¿Tiene cambio/billetes más pequeños?
teeyeh • neh kahm • beeyoh/bee • yeh • tehs mahs peh • keh • nyohs

Do you have change/ small bills [notes]?

Around…euros.	**Alrededor de los…euros.**
	ahl • reh • deh • dohr deh lohs…ew • rohs
Is it real?	**¿Es auténtico m/auténtica f?**
	ehs awoo • tehn • tee • koh/
	awoo • tehn • tee • kah
Can you show me this/that?	**¿Puede enseñarme esto/eso?**
	pweh • deh ehn • seh • nyahr • meh
	ehs • toh/eh • soh
That's not quite what I want.	**Eso no es realmente lo que busco.**
	eh • soh noh ehs reh • ahl • mehn • teh loh
	keh boos • koh
No, I don't like it.	**No, no me gusta.**
	noh noh meh goos • tah
It's too expensive.	**Es demasiado caro.**
	ehs deh • mah • seeyah • doh kah • roh
I have to think about it.	**Quiero pensármelo.**
	keeyeh • roh pehn • sahr • meh • loh
I'll take it.	**Me lo llevo.**
	meh loh yeh • boh

PAYING & BARGAINING

How much?	**¿Cuánto es?**
	kwahn • toh ehs
I'll pay…	**Voy a pagar…**
	boy ah pah • gahr…
in cash	**en efectivo**
	ehn eh • fehk • tee • boh
by credit card	**con tarjeta de crédito**
	kohn tahr • kheh • tah deh kreh • dee • toh
by traveler's check [cheque]	**con cheque de viaje**
	kohn cheh • keh deh beeyah • kheh
A receipt, please.	**Un recibo, por favor.**
	oon reh • thee • boh pohr fah • bohr

That's too much.	**Eso es demasiado.**
	_eh_ • _soh ehs deh_ • _mah_ • _seeyah_ • _doh_
I'll give you…	**Le doy…**
	leh doy…
I have only… euros.	**Sólo tengo…euros.**
	soh • _loh tehn_ • _goh…_ _ew_ • _rohs_
Is that your best price?	**¿Es el mejor precio que me puede hacer?**
	ehs ehl meh • _khohr preh_ • _theeyoh keh meh_
	pweh • _deh ah_ • _thehr_
Can you give me a discount?	**¿Puede hacerme un descuento?**
	pweh • _deh ah_ • _thehr_ • _meh oon_
	dehs • _kwehn_ • _toh_

MAKING A COMPLAINT

I'd like…	**Quiero…**
	keeyeh • _roh…_
to exchange this	**cambiar esto por otro**
	kahm • _beeyahr ehs_ • _toh pohr oh_ • _troh_
to return this	**devolver esto**
	deh • _bohl_ • _behr ehs_ • _toh_
a refund	**que me devuelvan el dinero**
	keh meh deh • _bwehl_ • _bahn ehl dee_ • _neh_ • _roh_

to see the manager	**hablar con el encargado** _ah • blahr kohn ehl ehn • kahr • gah • doh_

SERVICES

Can you recommend...?	**¿Puede recomendarme...?** _pweh • deh reh • koh • mehn • dahr • meh_
a barber	**una peluquería de caballeros** _oo • nah peh • loo • keh • ree • ah deh kah •_ _bah • yeh • rohs_
a dry cleaner	**una tintorería** _oo • nah teen • toh • reh • ree • ah_
a hairstylist	**una peluquería de señoras** _oo • nah peh • loo • keh • ree • ah deh seh •_ _nyoh • rahs_
a laundromat [launderette]	**una lavandería** _oo • nah lah • bahn • deh • ree • ah_
a nail salon	**un salón de manicura** _sah • lohn deh mah • nee • koo • rah_
a spa	**un centro de salud y belleza** _oon then • troh deh sah • lood_ _ee beh • yeh • thah_
a travel agency	**una agencia de viajes** _oo • nah ah • khehn • theeyah deh_ _beeyah • khehs_
Can you...this?	**¿Puede...esto?** _pweh • deh...ehs • toh_
alter	**hacerle un arreglo a** _ah • thehr • leh oon ah • rreh • gloh ah_
clean	**limpiar** _leem • peeyahr_
fix	**zurcir** _thoor • theer_
press	**planchar** _plahn • chahr_

When will it be ready?	**¿Cuándo estará listo?**
	kwahn • doh ehs • tah • rah lees • toh

HAIR & BEAUTY

I'd like…	**Quiero…**
	keeyeh • roh…
an appointment for today/tomorrow	**pedir hora para hoy/mañana**
	peh • deer oh • rah pah • rah oy/mah • nyah • nah
some color	**teñirme el pelo**
	teh • nyeer • meh ehl peh • loh
some highlights	**hacerme mechas**
	ah • thehr • meh meh • chahs
my hair styled/ blow-dried	**hacerme un peinado**
	ah • thehr • meh oon peyey • nah • doh
a haircut	**cortarme el pelo**
	kohr • tahr • meh ehl peh • loh
an eyebrow/ bikini wax	**depilarme las cejas/ingles**
	deh • pee • lahr • meh lahs theh • khahs/ een • glehs

(i)

With its varied landscapes and more than 2,000 registered springs (mineral and other), Spain is a prime location for spas, wellness centers and health-based resorts. These facilities offer a variety of treatments, including relaxation therapies and herbal remedies. Day spas can be found throughout the country, especially in the larger cities, and resort and overnight spas often offer individual services to those not staying there. Many of these also offer a wide variety of other relaxing activities such as horseback riding, guided tours, golf and swimming. Some spas and resorts do not allow children.

a facial	**hacerme una limpieza de cutis**
	ah • thehr • meh oo • nah leem • peeyeh • thah deh koo • tees
a manicure/ pedicure	**hacerme la manicura/pedicura**
	ah • thehr • meh lah mah • nee • koo • rah/ peh • dee • koo • rah
a (sports) massage	**un masaje (deportivo)**
	oon mah • sah • kheh (deh • pohr • tee • boh)
a trim	**cortarme las puntas**
	kohr • tahr • meh lahs poon • tahs
Not too short.	**No me lo corte demasiado.**
	noh meh loh kohr • teh deh • mah • seeyah • doh
Shorter here.	**Quíteme más de aquí.**
	kee • teh • meh mahs deh ah • kee
Do you offer…?	**¿Hacen…?**
	ah • thehn…
acupuncture	**acupuntura**
	ah • koo • poon • too • rah
aromatherapy	**aromaterapia**
	ah • roh • mah • teh • rah • peeyah
oxygen treatment	**oxígenoterapia**
	oh • xee • kheh • noh • teh • rah • peeyah

Do you have a sauna?	**¿Tienen una sauna?** _teeyehn • ehn <u>oo</u> • nah <u>sawoo</u> • nah_

ANTIQUES

How old is it?	**¿Qué antigüedad tiene?** _keh ahn • tee • gweh • <u>dahd</u> <u>teeyeh</u> • neh_
Do you have anything from the…period?	**¿Tiene algo de la época…?** _teeyeh • neh <u>ahl</u> • goh deh lah eh • poh • kah…_
Do I have to fill out any forms?	**¿Tengo que rellenar algún impreso?** _tehn • goh keh reh • yeh • <u>nahr</u> ahl • <u>goon</u> eem • <u>preh</u> • soh_
Is there a certificate of authenticity?	**¿Tiene el certificado de autenticidad?** _teeyeh • neh ehl thehr • tee • fee • <u>kah</u> • doh deh awoo • tehn • tee • thee • <u>dahd</u>_
Can you ship/wrap it?	**¿Puede llevármelo/envolvérmelo?** _pweh • deh yeh • bahr • meh • loh/ ehn • bohl • behr • meh • loh_

CLOTHING

I'd like…	**Quiero…** _keeyeh • roh…_
Can I try this on?	**¿Puedo probarme esto?** _pweh • doh proh • <u>bahr</u> • meh ehs • toh_

YOU MAY HEAR…

Le queda genial _leh keh • dah kheh • neeyahl_	That looks great on you.
¿Cómo le queda? _koh • moh meh khe • dah_	How does it fit?
No tenemos su talla _noh teh • neh • mohs soo tah • yah_	We don't have your size.

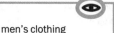

YOU MAY SEE…

ROPA DE CABALLERO	men's clothing
ROPA DE SEÑORA	women's clothing
ROPA DE NIÑOS	children's clothing

It doesn't fit.	**No me queda bien.**
	noh meh keh•dah beeyehn
It's too…	**Me queda demasiado…**
	meh keh•dah deh•mah•seeyah•doh…
big/small	**grande/pequeño** m/**pequeña** f
	grahn•deh/peh•keh•nyoh/
	peh•keh•nyah
short/long	**corto** m/**corta** f/**largo** m/**larga** f
	kohr•toh/kohr•tah/lahr•goh/lahr•gah
tight/loose	**ajustado/ancho**
	ah•khoos•tah•doh/ahn•choh
Do you have this in size…?	**¿Tiene esto en la talla…?**
	teeyeh•neh ehs•toh ehn lah tah•yah…
Do you have this in a bigger/ smaller size?	**¿Tiene esto en una talla más grande/ pequeña?**
	teeyeh•neh ehs•toh ehn oo•nah tah•yah mahs grahn•deh/peh•keh•nyah

COLORS

I'd like something…	**Busco algo…**
	boos•koh ahl•goh…
beige	**beis**
	behyees
black	**negro**
	neh•groh
blue	**azul**
	ah•thool

brown	**marrón**
	mah • rrohn
green	**verde**
	behr • deh
gray	**gris**
	grees
orange	**naranja**
	nah • rahn • khah
pink	**rosa**
	roh • sah
purple	**morado**
	moh • rah • doh
red	**rojo**
	roh • khoh
white	**blanco**
	blahn • koh
yellow	**amarillo**
	ah • mah • ree • yoh

CLOTHES & ACCESSORIES

a backpack	**la mochila**
	lah moh • chee • lah
a belt	**el cinturón**
	ehl theen • too • rohn
a bikini	**el bikini**
	ehl bee • kee • nee
a blouse	**la blusa**
	lah bloo • sah
a bra	**el sujetador**
	ehl soo • kheh • tah • dohr
briefs/panties	**los calzoncillos/las bragas**
	lohs kahl • thohn • thee • yohs/lahs brah • gahs
a coat	**el abrigo**
	ehl ah • bree • goh

a dress	**el vestido**
	ehl behs • tee • doh
a hat	**el sombrero**
	ehl sohm • breh • roh
a jacket	**la chaqueta**
	lah chah • keh • tah
jeans	**los vaqueros**
	lohs bah • keh • rohs
pajamas	**el pijama**
	ehl pee • khah • mah
pants [trousers]	**los pantalones**
	lohs pahn • tah • loh • nehs
pantyhose [tights]	**las medias**
	lahs meh • deeyahs
a purse [handbag]	**el bolso**
	ehl bohl • soh
a raincoat	**el impermeable**
	ehl eem • pehr • meh • ah • bleh
a scarf	**la bufanda**
	lah boo • fahn • dah
a shirt	**la camisa**
	lah kah • mee • sah
shorts	**los pantalones cortos**
	lohs pahn • tah • loh • nehs kohr • tohs
a skirt	**la falda**
	lah fahl • dah
socks	**los calcetines**
	lohs kahl • theh • tee • nehs
a suit	**el traje de chaqueta**
	ehl trah • kheh deh chah • keh • tah
sunglasses	**las gafas de sol**
	lahs gah • fahs deh sohl
a sweater	**el jersey**
	ehl khehr • seyee
a sweatshirt	**la sudadera**

	lah soo • dah • <u>deh</u> • rah
a swimsuit	**el bañador**
	ehl bah • nyah • <u>dohr</u>
a T-shirt	**la camiseta**
	lah kah • mee • <u>seh</u> • tah
a tie	**la corbata**
	lah kohr • <u>bah</u> • tah
underwear	**la ropa interior**
	lah <u>roh</u> • pah een • teh • <u>reeyohr</u>

FABRIC

I'd like…	**Quiero…**
	<u>keeyeh</u> • roh…
cotton	**algodón**
	ahl • goh • <u>dohn</u>
denim	**tela vaquera**
	<u>teh</u> • lah bah • <u>keh</u> • rah
lace	**encaje**
	ehn • <u>kah</u> • kheh
leather	**cuero**
	<u>kweh</u> • roh
linen	**lino**
	<u>lee</u> • noh

silk	**seda**
	seh • dah
wool	**lana**
	lah • nah
Is it machine washable?	**¿Se puede lavar a máquina?**
	seh pweh • deh lah • bahr ah mah • kee • nah

SHOES

I'd like…	**Quiero…**
	keeyeh • roh…
high-heels/flats	**zapatos de tacón/planos**
	thah • pah • tohs deh tah • kohn/plah • nohs
boots	**botas**
	boh • tahs
loafers	**mocasines**
	moh • kah • see • nehs
sandals	**sandalias**
	sahn • dah • leeyahs
shoes	**zapatos**
	thah • pah • tohs
slippers	**zapatillas**
	thah • pah • tee • yahs
sneakers	**zapatillas de deporte**
	thah • pah • tee • yahs deh deh • pohr • teh
In size…	**En la talla…**
	ehn lah tah • yah…

For Numbers, see page 20.

SIZES

small (S)	**pequeña (P)** *peh • keh • nyah (peh)*
medium (M)	**mediana (M)** *meh • deeyah • nah (ehm)*
large (L)	**grande (G)** *grahn • deh (kheh)*
extra large (XL)	**XL** *ehkees • ehleh*
petite	**tallas pequeñas** *tah • yahs peh • keh • nyahs*
plus size	**tallas grandes** *tah • yahs grahn • dehs*

NEWSAGENT & TOBACCONIST

Do you sell English-language newspapers?	**¿Venden periódicos en inglés?** *behn • dehn peh • reeyoh • dee • kohs ehn een • glehs*
I'd like…	**Quiero…** *keeyeh • roh…*
candy [sweets]	**caramelos** *kah • rah • meh • lohs*
chewing gum	**chicle** *chee • kleh*
a chocolate bar	**una chocolatina** *oo • nah choh • koh • lah • tee • nah*
a cigar	**un puro** *oon poo • roh*
a pack/carton of cigarettes	**un paquete/cartón de tabaco** *oon pah • keh • teh/kahr • tohn deh tah • bah • koh*

a lighter	**un mechero**
	oon meh • cheh • roh
a magazine	**una revista**
	oo • nah reh • bees • tah
matches	**cerillas** *theh • ree • yahs*
a newspaper	**un periódico**
	oon peh • reeyoh • dee • koh
a pen	**un bolígrafo**
	oon boh • lee • grah • foh
a postcard	**una postal**
	oo • nah pohs • tahl
a road/town	**un mapa de las carreteras/plano de...**
map of...	*oon mah • pah deh lahs kah • rreh • teh •*
	rahs/plah • noh deh...
stamps	**sellos** *seh • yohs*

PHOTOGRAPHY

I'd like a/an...	**Quiero una cámara...**
camera.	*keeyeh • roh oo • nah kah • mah • rah...*
automatic	**automática**
	awoo • toh • mah • tee • kah
digital	**digital**
	dee • khee • tahl
disposable	**desechable**
	deh • seh • chah • bleh
I'd like...	**Quiero...**
	keeyeh • roh...
a battery	**una pila**
	oo • nah pee • lah
digital prints	**fotos digitales**
	foh • tohs dee • khee • tah • lehs
a memory card	**una tarjeta de memoria**
	oo • nah tahr • kheh • tah deh
	meh • moh • reeyah

Can I print digital photos here?	**¿Puedo imprimir aquí fotos digitales?** _pweh • doh eem • pree • meer ah • kee foh • tohs dee • khee • tah • lehs_

SOUVENIRS

bottle of wine	**la botella de vino** _lah boh • teh • yah deh bee • noh_
box of chocolates	**la caja de bombones** _lah kah • khah deh bohm • boh • nehs_
castanets	**las castañuelas** _lahs kahs • tah • nyweh • lahs_
doll	**la muñeca** _lah moo • nyeh • kah_
fan (wooden, flamenco)	**el abanico de madera** _ehl ah • bah • nee • koh deh mah • deh • rah_
key ring	**el llavero** _ehl yah • beh • roh_

Spain produces a wide range of souvenirs, from typical tourist T-shirts to high-quality regional crafts. Spanish wine is popular and quality examples, such as sherry from Jerez and red wine from Rioja, can be found all over. Olive oil is also a popular gift. Classic Spanish souvenirs include bullfighting mementos, such as figurines, posters or capes, castanets, hand-painted flamenco fans and guitars. Reproduction paintings by Spain's most famous artists, such as Picasso, Dalí, Miró, Goya, El Greco or Velázquez, are also popular. Specialty regional goods include copperware, earthenware, leather goods, jewelry, lace, porcelain and wood carvings. Spanish swords and other metal work from Toledo are unique gifts, and Lladro® porcelain figurines are very popular.

postcard	**la postal**
	lah pohs • tahl
pottery	**la cerámica**
	lah theh • rah • mee • kah
serrano ham	**el jamón serrano**
	ehl khah • mohn seh • rrah • noh
T-shirt	**la camiseta**
	lah kah • mee • seh • tah
terracotta bowl	**la cazuela de barro**
	lah kah • thweh • lah deh bah • rroh
toy	**el juguete**
	ehl khoo • geh • teh
wine	**el vino**
	ehl bee • noh
Can I see this/that?	**¿Puedo ver esto/eso?**
	pweh • doh behr ehs • toh/eh • soh
It's in the window/ display case.	**Está en el escaparate/la vitrina.**
	ehs • tah ehn ehl ehs • kah • pah • rah • teh/ lah bee • tree • nah
I'd like…	**Quiero…**
	keeyeh • roh…
a battery	**una pila**
	oo • nah pee • lah
a bracelet	**una pulsera**
	oo • nah pool • seh • rah
a brooch	**un broche**
	oon broh • cheh
earrings	**unos pendientes**
	oo • nohs pehn • deeyehn • tehs
a necklace	**un collar**
	oon koh • yahr
a ring	**un anillo**
	oon ah • nee • yoh
a watch	**un reloj de pulsera**
	oon reh • lohkh deh pool • seh • rah

I'd like...	**Quiero...**
	keeyeh • roh...
copper	**cobre**
	koh • breh
crystal	**cristal**
	krees • tahl
diamonds	**diamantes**
	deeyah • mahn • tehs
white/yellow gold	**oro blanco/amarillo**
	oh • roh blahn • koh/ah • mah • ree • yoh
pearls	**perlas**
	pehr • lahs
pewter	**peltre**
	pehl • treh
platinum	**platino**
	plah • tee • noh
sterling silver	**plata esterlina**
	plah • tah ehs • tehr • lee • nah
Is this real?	**¿Es auténtico?**
	ehs awoo • tehn • tee • koh
Can you engrave it?	**¿Puede grabármelo?**
	pweh • deh grah • bahr • meh • loh

SPORT & LEISURE

NEED TO KNOW

When's the game?	**¿Cuándo empieza el partido?** _kwahn_ • doh ehm • _peeyeh_ • thah ehl pahr • _tee_ • doh
Where's…?	**¿Dónde está…?** _dohn_ • deh ehs • _tah_…
the beach	**la playa** lah _plah_ • yah
the park	**el parque** ehl _pahr_ • keh
the pool	**la piscina** lah pees • _thee_ • nah
Is it safe to swim here?	**¿Es seguro nadar aquí?** ehs seh • _goo_ • roh nah • _dahr_ ah • _kee_
Can I rent [hire] golf clubs?	**¿Puedo alquilar palos de golf?** _pweh_ • doh ahl • kee • _lahr pah_ • lohs deh golf
How much per hour?	**¿Cuánto cuesta por hora?** _kwahn_ • toh _kwehs_ • tah pohr _oh_ • rah

How far is it to…?	**¿A qué distancia está…?** *ah keh dees • tahn • theeyah ehs • tah…*
Can you show me on the map, please?	**¿Puede indicármelo en el mapa, por favor?** *pweh • deh een • dee • kahr • meh • loh ehn ehl mah • pah pohr fah • bohr*

WATCHING SPORT

When's…?	**¿Cuándo empieza…?** *kwahn • doh ehm • peeyeh • thah…*
the baseball game	**el juego del béisbol** *ehl khooeh • goh dehl behees • bohl*
the basketball game	**el partido de baloncesto** *ehl pahr • tee • doh deh bah • lohn • thehs • toh*
the boxing match	**la pelea de boxeo** *lah peh • leh • ah deh bohks • eh • oh*
the cycling race	**la vuelta ciclista** *lah bwehl • tah thee • klees • tah*
the golf tournament	**el torneo de golf** *ehl tohr • neh • oh deh golf*
the soccer [football] game	**el partido de fútbol** *ehl pahr • tee • doh deh foot • bohl*
the tennis match	**el partido de tenis** *ehl pahr • tee • doh deh teh • nees*
the volleyball game	**el partido de voleibol** *ehl pahr • tee • doh deh boh • leyee • bohl*
Who's playing?	**¿Quienes juegan?** *keeyeh • nehs khweh • gahn*
Where is…?	**¿Dónde está…?** *dohn • deh ehs • tah…*
the horsetrack	**el hipódromo** *ehl ee • poh • droh • moh*

the racetrack	**el circuito de carreras**
	ehl theer • kwee • toh de kah • rreh • rahs
the stadium	**el estadio**
	ehl ehs • tah • deeyoh
Where can I place a bet?	**¿Dónde puedo hacer una apuesta?**
	dohn • deh pweh • doh ah • thehr oo • nah ah • pwehs • tah

PLAYING SPORT

Where is/are…?	**¿Dónde está/están…?**
	dohn • deh ehs • tah/ehs • tahn…
the golf course	**el campo de golf**
	ehl kahm • poh deh golf
the gym	**el gimnasio**
	ehl kheem • nah • seeyoh
the park	**el parque**
	ehl pahr • keh

Fútbol (soccer) is the most popular sport in Spain; most cities in Spain have their own professional teams with a large fan base. Note that fans are extremely dedicated, so be sure not to insult the team. Almost all activity in Spain stops when there is an important soccer game on.

Golf is also popular and the golf courses on the Costa del Sol are worth a round. Other popular sports include basketball, tennis, auto racing, horse racing, hiking and climbing. **Jai alai** is a popular fast-paced game involving balls and curved-wicker-basket gloves.

There are many casinos throughout Spain. Minimum entrance and gaming age is 18; ID is required and the dress code is business casual.

the tennis courts	**las canchas de tenis**
	lahs kahn • chahs deh teh • nees
How much per...?	**¿Cuánto cuesta por...?**
	kwahn • toh kwehs • tah pohr...
day	**día**
	dee • ah
hour	**hora**
	oh • rah
game	**partido**
	pahr • tee • doh
round	**juego**
	khweh • goh
Can I rent [hire]...?	**¿Puedo alquilar...?**
	pweh • doh ahl • kee • lahr...
golf clubs	**palos de golf**
	pah • lohs deh golf
equipment	**equipo**
	eh • kee • poh
a racket	**una raqueta**
	oo • nah rah • keh • tah

AT THE BEACH/POOL

Where's the beach/pool?	**¿Dónde está la playa/piscina?**
	dohn • deh ehs • tah lah plah • yah/ pees • thee • nah
Is there...?	**¿Hay...?**
	aye...
a kiddie pool	**una piscina infantil**
	oo • nah pees • thee • nah een • fahn • teel
an indoor/ outdoor pool	**una piscina cubierta/exterior**
	oo • nah pees • thee • nah koo • beeyehr • tah/ehx • teh • reeyohr
a lifeguard	**un socorrista**
	oon soh • koh • rrees • tah

Is it safe…?	**¿Es seguro…?**
	ehs seh • goo • roh…
to swim	**nadar**
	nah • dahr
to dive	**tirarse de cabeza**
	tee • rahr • seh deh kah • beh • thah
for children	**para los niños**
	pah • rah lohs nee • nyohs
I'd like to hire…	**Quiero alquilar…**
	keeyeh • roh ahl • kee • lahr…
a deck chair	**una tumbona**
	oo • nah toom • boh • nah
diving equipment	**equipo de buceo**
	eh • kee • poh deh boo • theh • oh
a jet ski	**una moto acuática**
	oo • nah moh • toh ah • kwah • tee • kah
a motorboat	**una lancha motora**
	oo • nah lahn • chah moh • toh • rah
a rowboat	**una barca de remos**
	oo • nah bahr • kah deh reh • mohs
snorkeling equipment	**equipo de esnórquel**
	eh • kee • poh deh ehs • nohr • kehl
a surfboard	**una tabla de surf**
	oo • nah tah • blah deh soorf
a towel	**una toalla**
	oo • nah toh • ah • yah
an umbrella	**una sombrilla**
	oo • nah sohm • bree • yah
water skis	**unos esquís acuáticos**
	oo • nohs ehs • kees ah • kwah • tee • kohs
a windsurfer	**una tabla de windsurf**
	oo • nah tah • blah deh weend • soorf
For…hours.	**Por…horas.**
	pohr…oh • rahs

WINTER SPORTS

A lift pass for a day/five days, please.	**Un pase de un día/cinco días de acceso a los remontes.** *oon pah•seh deh oon dee•ah/theen•koh dee•ahs deh ahk•theh•soh ah lohs reh•mohn•tehs*
I'd like to hire [hire]…	**Quiero alquilar…** *keeyeh•roh ahl•kee•lahr…*
boots	**botas** *boh•tahs*
a helmet	**un casco** *oon kahs•koh*
poles	**bastones** *bahs•toh•nehs*
skis	**esquís** *ehs•kees*
a snowboard	**una tabla de snowboard** *oo•nah tah•blah deh snoh•bohrd*
snowshoes	**raquetas de nieve** *rah•keh•tahs deh neeyeh•beh*
Are there lessons?	**¿Dan clases?** *dahn klah•sehs*

These are too big/small.	**Me quedan demasiado grandes/ pequeños.**
	meh keh • dahn deh • mah • seeyah • doh grahn • dehs/peh • keh • nyohs
I'm a beginner.	**Soy principiante.**
	soy preen • thee • peeyahn • teh
I'm experienced.	**Tengo experiencia.**
	tehn • goh ehx • peh • reeyehn • theeyah
A trail [piste] map, please.	**Un mapa de las pistas, por favor.**
	oon mah • pah deh lahs pees • tahs pohr fah • bohr

OUT IN THE COUNTRY

A map of…, please.	**Un mapa de…, por favor.**
	oon mah • pah deh… pohr fah • bohr
this region	**esta región**
	ehs • tah reh • kheeyohn
the walking routes	**las rutas de senderismo**
	lahs roo • tahs deh sehn • deh • rees • moh
the bike routes	**los senderos para bicicletas**
	lohs sehn • deh • rohs pah • rah bee • thee • kleh • tahs

(i)

Spain has more than 2,400 miles (4,000 km) of coastline and more than 1,700 beaches, with 16 different **Costas** (coastal regions). Two of the more famous coastal regions are **Costa del Sol** and **Costa Blanca**. Spain's Balearic and Canary Islands boast some of the most beautiful beaches in the world. If you decide to go for a swim, check the safety flags at each beach. Green flags indicate the water is safe, yellow flags indicate that you should use caution and red flags indicate that the water is unsafe for swimming.

ⓘ

Spain has three mountain ranges, the Pyrenees, the
Sierra Nevada and the Cantabrian, with an average altitude
of 2,000 feet (600 m). There are more than 30 ski resorts
throughout Spain with more than 620 miles (1,000 km) of
ski runs combined. In addition to skiing, most resorts and
ski areas offer other winter activities such as snowboarding,
snowmobiling, sledding and dog-sledding.

the trails	**los senderos**
	lohs sehn•deh•rohs
Is it… easy/difficult?	**¿Es… fácil/difícil?**
	ehs fah•theel/dee•fee•theel
Is it far/steep?	**¿Está lejos/empinado?**
	ehs•tah leh•khohs/ehm•pee•nah•doh
I'm lost.	**Me he perdido.**
	meh eh pehr•dee•doh
How far is it to…?	**¿A qué distancia está…?**
	ah keh dees•tahn•theeah ehs•tah…
Can you show me on the map, please?	**¿Puede indicármelo en el mapa, por favor?**
	pweh•deh een•dee•kahr•meh•loh ehn ehl mah•pah pohr fah•bohr

👁

YOU MAY SEE…

TELESQUÍ	drag lift
TELEFÉRICO	cable car
TELESILLA	chair lift
PRINCIPIANTE	novice
NIVEL INTERMEDIO	intermediate
EXPERTO	expert
PISTA CERRADA	trail [piste] closed

Where is…?	**¿Dónde está…?**
	dohn • deh ehs • _tah_…
the bridge	**el puente**
	ehl _pwehn_ • teh
the cave	**la cueva**
	lah _kweh_ • bah
the cliff	**el acantilado**
	ehl ah • kahn • tee • _lah_ • doh
the desert	**el desierto**
	ehl deh • _seeyehr_ • toh
the farm	**la granja**
	lah _grahn_ • khah
the field	**el campo**
	ehl _kahm_ • poh
the forest	**el bosque**
	ehl _bohs_ • keh
the hill	**la colina**
	lah koh • _lee_ • nah
the lake	**el lago**
	ehl _lah_ • goh
the mountain	**la montaña**
	lah mohn • _tah_ • nyah
the nature preserve	**la reserva natural**
	lah reh • _sehr_ • bah nah • too • _rahl_
the viewpoint	**el mirador**
	ehl mee • rah • _dohr_
the park	**el parque**
	ehl _pahr_ • keh
the path	**el camino**
	ehl kah • _mee_ • noh
the peak	**el pico**
	ehl _pee_ • koh
the picnic area	**la zona de picnic**
	lah _thoh_ • nah deh peek • _neek_

the pond	**el estanque**
	ehl ehs • <u>tahn</u> • keh
the river	**el río**
	ehl <u>ree</u> • oh
the sea	**el mar**
	ehl mahr
the (thermal)	**el manantial (de aguas termales)**
spring	*ehl mah • nahn • <u>teeyahl</u> (deh <u>ah</u> • gwahs*
	tehr • <u>mah</u> • lehs)
the stream	**el arroyo**
	ehl ah • <u>rroh</u> • yoh
the valley	**el valle**
	ehl <u>bah</u> • yeh
the vineyard	**la viña**
	lah <u>bee</u> • nyah
the waterfall	**la cascada**
	lah kahs • <u>kah</u> • dah

For Asking Directions, see page 61.

TRAVELING WITH CHILDREN

NEED TO KNOW

Is there a discount for kids?	**¿Hacen descuento a niños?**
	_ah_ • then dehs • _kwehn_ • toh ah _nee_ • nyohs
Can you recommend a babysitter?	**¿Puede recomendarme una canguro?**
	pweh • deh eh • koh • mehn • _dahr_ • meh oo • nah kahn • _goo_ • roh
Do you have a child's seat/highchair?	**¿Tienen una silla para niños/trona?**
	teeyeh • nehn oo • nah see • yah pah • rah _nee_ • nyohs/_troh_ • nah
Where can I change the baby?	**¿Dónde puedo cambiar al bebé?**
	dohn • deh _pweh_ • doh kahm • _beeyahr_ ahl beh • _beh_

OUT & ABOUT

Can you recommend something for kids?	**¿Puede recomendarme algo para los niños?**
	pweh • deh reh • koh • mehn • _dahr_ • meh _ahl_ • goh pah • rah lohs nee • nyohs

Where's…?	¿Dónde está…?
	dohn • deh ehs • tah…
the amusement park	**el parque de atracciones**
	ehl pahr • keh deh ah • trahk • theeyoh • nehs
the arcade	**el salón de juegos recreativos**
	ehl sah • lohn deh khweh • gohs reh • kreh • ah • tee • bohs
the kiddie [paddling] pool	**la piscina infantil**
	lah pees • thee • nah een • fahn • teel
the park	**el parque**
	ehl pahr • keh
the playground	**el parque infantil**
	ehl pahr • keh een • fahn • teel
the zoo	**el zoológico**
	ehl thoh • oh • loh • khee • koh
Are kids allowed?	**¿Se permite la entrada a niños?**
	she pehr • mee • teh lah ehn • trah • dah ah nee • nyohs
Is it safe for kids?	**¿Es seguro para niños?**
	ehs seh • goo • roh pah • rah nee • nyohs
Is it suitable for… year olds?	**¿Es apto para niños de…años?**
	ehs ahp • toh pah • rah nee • nyohs deh… ah • nyohs

For Numbers, see page 20.

YOU MAY HEAR…

¡Qué mono m/mona f!	How cute!
keh moh • noh/moh • nah	
¿Cómo se llama?	What's
koh • moh seh yah • mah	his/her name?
¿Qué edad tiene?	How old is
keh eh • dahth teeyeh • neh	he/she?

BABY ESSENTIALS

Do you have…?	**¿Tiene…?**
	teeyeh • neh…
a baby bottle	**un biberón**
	oon bee • beh • <u>rohn</u>
baby food	**la papilla**
	lah papeeyah
baby wipes	**toallitas**
	toh • ah • <u>yee</u> • tahs
a car seat	**un asiento para niños**
	oon ah • <u>seeyehn</u> toh <u>pah</u> • rah <u>nee</u> • nyohs
a children's menu/portion	**un menú/una ración para niños**
	oon meh • <u>noo</u>/<u>oo</u> • nah rah • <u>theeyohn</u> <u>pah</u> • rah <u>nee</u> • nyohs
a child's seat/highchair	**una silla para niños/trona**
	<u>oo</u> • nah <u>see</u> • yah <u>pah</u> • rah <u>nee</u> • nyohs/ <u>troh</u> • nah
a crib/cot	**una cuna/un catre**
	<u>oo</u> • nah <u>koo</u> • nah/oon <u>kah</u> • treh
diapers [nappies]	**pañales**
	pah • <u>nyah</u> • lehs
formula	**fórmula infantil**
	<u>fohr</u> • moo • lah een • fahn • <u>teel</u>
a pacifier [dummy]	**un chupete**
	oon choo • <u>peh</u> • teh

a playpen	**un parque** *oon pahr • keh*
a stroller [pushchair]	**un cochecito** *oon koh • cheh • thee • toh*
Can I breastfeed the baby here?	**¿Puedo darle el pecho al bebé aquí?** *pweh • doh dahr • leh ehl peh • choh ahl beh • beh ah • kee*
Where can I change the baby?	**¿Dónde puedo cambiar al bebé?** *dohn • deh pweh • doh kahm • beeyahr ahl beh • beh*

BABYSITTING

Can you recommend a babysitter?	**¿Puede recomendarme una canguro?** *pweh • deh reh • koh • mehn • dahr • meh oo • nah kahn • goo • roh*
How much do they charge?	**¿Cuánto cuesta?** *kwahn • toh kwehs • tah*
I'll be back by…	**Vuelvo a la/las…** *bwehl • boh ah lah/lahs…*
If you need to contact me, call…	**Puede contactarme en el…** *pweh • deh kohn • tahk • tahr • meh ehn ehl…*

For Grammar, see page 12.

HEALTH & SAFETY

EMERGENCIES

NEED TO KNOW

Help!	**¡Socorro!**
	soh • <u>koh</u> • rroh
Go away!	**¡Lárguese!**
	<u>lahr</u> • geh • seh
Stop, thief!	**¡Deténgase, ladrón!**
	deh • <u>tehn</u> • gah • seh lah • <u>drohn</u>
Get a doctor!	**¡Llame a un médico!**
	<u>yah</u> • meh ah oon <u>meh</u> • dee • koh
Fire!	**¡Fuego!**
	<u>fweh</u> • goh
I'm lost.	**Me he perdido.**
	meh eh pehr • <u>dee</u> • doh
Can you help me?	**¿Puede ayudarme?**
	<u>pweh</u> • deh ah • yoo • <u>dahr</u> • meh

In an emergency, dial: **112** for the police
080 for the fire brigade
061 for the ambulance.

YOU MAY HEAR...

Rellene este impreso.
reh • yeh • neh ehs • teh eem • preh • soh
Fill out this form.

Su documento de identidad, por favor.
soo doh • koo • mehn • toh deh ee • dehn • tee • dahd pohr fah • bohr
Your identification, please.

¿Cuándo/Dónde ocurrió?
kwahn • doh/dohn • deh oh • koo • rreeyoh
When/Where did it happen?

¿Puede describirle?/describirla?
pweh • deh dehs • kree • beer • leh?/ dehs • kree • beer • lah?
What does he/she look like?

POLICE

NEED TO KNOW

Call the police!	**¡Llame a la policía!** *yah • meh ah lah poh • lee • thee • ah*
Where's the police station?	**¿Dónde está la comisaría?** *dohn • deh ehs • tah lah koh • mee • sah • ree • ah*
There was an accident/attack.	**Ha habido un accidente/asalto.** *ah ah • bee • doh oon ahk • thee • dehn • teh/ah • sahl • toh*
My son/daughter is missing.	**Mi hijo m/hija f ha desaparecido.** *mee ee • khoh/ee • khah ah deh •*

	sah • pah • reh • <u>thee</u> • doh
I need…	**Necesito…**
	neh • theh • <u>see</u> • toh…
an interpreter	**un intérprete**
	oon een • <u>tehr</u> • preh • teh
to contact	**ponerme en contacto con mi abogado**
my lawyer	_poh • <u>nehr</u> • meh ehn kohn • <u>tahk</u> • toh_
	kohn mee ah • boh • <u>gah</u> • doh
to make a	**hacer una llamada**
phone call	_ah • <u>thehr</u> <u>oo</u> • nah yah • <u>mah</u> • dah_
I'm innocent.	**Soy inocente.**
	soy ee • noh • <u>thehn</u> • teh

CRIME & LOST PROPERTY

I want to report…	**Quiero denunciar…**
	<u>keeyeh</u> • roh deh • noon • <u>theeyahr</u>…
a mugging	**un asalto**
	oon ah • <u>sahl</u> • toh
a rape	**una violación**
	<u>oo</u> • nah beeyoh • lah • <u>theeyohn</u>
a theft	**un robo**
	oon <u>roh</u> • boh
I've been mugged/	**Me han asaltado/atracado.**
robbed.	_meh ahn ah • sahl • <u>tah</u> • doh/_
	ah • trah • <u>kah</u> • doh
I've lost my…	**He perdido…**
	eh pehr • <u>dee</u> • doh…
My…was stolen.	**Me han robado…**
	meh ahn • roh • <u>bah</u> • doh…
backpack	**la mochila**
	lah moh • <u>chee</u> • lah
bicycle	**la bicicleta**
	lah bee • thee • <u>kleh</u> • tah

camera	**la cámara**
	lah <u>kah</u> • mah • rah
(hire) car	**el coche (de alquiler)**
	ehl <u>koh</u> • cheh (deh ahl • kee • <u>lehr</u>)
computer	**el ordenador**
	ehl ohr • deh • nah • <u>dohr</u>
credit card	**la tarjeta de crédito**
	lah tahr • <u>kheh</u> • tah deh <u>kreh</u> • dee • toh
jewelry	**las joyas**
	lahs <u>khoh</u> • yahs
money	**el dinero**
	ehl dee • <u>neh</u> • roh
passport	**el pasaporte**
	ehl pah • sah • <u>pohr</u> • teh
purse [handbag]	**el bolso**
	ehl <u>bohl</u> • soh
traveler's	**los cheques de viaje**
	lohs <u>cheh</u> • kehs deh
cheques	*<u>beeyah</u> • kheh*
wallet	**la cartera**
	lah kahr • <u>teh</u> • rah
I need a police report.	**Necesito un certificado de la policía.**
	neh • theh • <u>see</u> • toh oon thehr • tee •
	fee • <u>kah</u> • doh deh lah poh • lee • <u>thee</u> • ah

Where is the British/ American/Irish embassy?	**¿Dónde está la embajada británica/ americana/irlandesa?** *dohn • deh ehs • tah lah ehm • bah • khah • dah bree • tah • nee • kah/ah • meh • ree • kah • nah/ eer • lahn • deh • sah*

HEALTH

NEED TO KNOW

I'm sick [ill].	**Me encuentro mal.** *meh ehn • kwehn • troh mahl*
I need an English-speaking doctor.	**Necesito un médico que hable inglés.** *neh • theh • see • toh oon meh • dee • koh keh ah • bleh een • glehs*
It hurts here.	**Me duele aquí.** *meh dweh • leh ah • kee*
I have a stomachache.	**Tengo dolor de estómago.** *tehn • goh doh • lohr deh ehs • toh • mah • goh*

FINDING A DOCTOR

Can you recommend a doctor/dentist?	**¿Puede recomendarme un médico/ dentista?** *pweh • deh reh • koh • mehn • dahr • meh oon meh • dee • koh/ dehn • tees • tah*
Can the doctor come here?	**¿Podría el médico venir aquí?** *poh • dree • ah ehl meh • dee • koh beh • neer ah • kee*

I need an English-speaking doctor.	**Necesito un médico que hable inglés.** *neh • theh • <u>see</u> • toh oon <u>meh</u> • dee • koh keh* *ah • bleh een • <u>glehs</u>*
What are the office hours?	**¿Cuáles son las horas de consulta?** *<u>kwah</u> • lehs sohn lahs <u>oh</u> • rahs deh kohn •* *<u>sool</u> • tah*
I'd like an appointment…	**Quiero una cita…** *<u>keeyeh</u> • roh oo • nah <u>thee</u> • tah…*
for today	**para hoy** *<u>pah</u> • rah ohy*
for tomorrow	**para mañana** *<u>pah</u> • rah mah • <u>nyah</u> • nah*
as soon as possible	**lo antes posible** *loh <u>ahn</u> • tehs poh • <u>see</u> • bleh*
It's urgent.	**Es urgente.** *ehs oor • <u>khehn</u> • teh*

SYMPTOMS

I'm…	**Estoy…** *ehs • <u>toy</u>…*
bleeding	**sangrando** *sahn • <u>grahn</u> • doh*
constipated	**estreñido** *m*/**estreñida** *f* *ehs • treh • <u>nyee</u> • doh/ehs • treh • <u>nyee</u> • dah*
dizzy	**mareado** *m*/**mareada** *f* *mah • reh • <u>ah</u> • doh/mah • reh • <u>ah</u> • dah*
I'm nauseous	**Tengo náuseas.** *<u>tehn</u> • goh <u>naw</u> • seh • ahs*
I'm vomiting.	**Tengo vómitos.** *<u>tehn</u> • goh <u>boh</u> • mee • tohs*
It hurts here.	**Me duele aquí.** *meh <u>dweh</u> • leh ah • <u>kee</u>*
I have…	**Tengo…** *<u>tehn</u> • goh…*

YOU MAY HEAR...

¿Qué le pasa?
keh leh pah • sah
What's wrong?

¿Dónde le duele?
dohn • deh leh dweh • leh
Where does it hurt?

¿Le duele aquí?
leh dweh • leh ah • kee
Does it hurt here?

¿Esta tomando algún medicamento?
ehs • tah toh • mahn • doh ahl • goon meh • dee • kah • mehn • toh
Are you on medication?

¿Es alérgico m/alérgica f a algo?
ehs ah • lehr • khee • koh/ah • lehr • khee • kah ah ahl • goh
Are you allergic to anything?

Abra la boca.
ah • brah lah boh • kah
Open your mouth.

Respire hondo.
rehs • pee • reh ohn • doh
Breathe deeply.

Tiene que ir al hospital.
teeyeh • neh keh eer ahl ohs • pee • tahl
You/he/she must go to the hospital.

an allergic reaction	**una reacción alérgica**
	oo • nah reh • ahk • theeyohn ah • lehr • khee • kah
chest pain	**dolor de pecho**
	doh • lohr deh peh • choh
cramps	**calambres**
	kah • lahm • brehs
diarrhea	**diarrea**
	deeyah • rreh • ah
an earache	**dolor de oído**
	doh • lohr deh oh • ee • doh
a fever	**fiebre**
	feeyeh • breh

pain	**dolor**
	doh • lohr
a rash	**una erupción cutánea**
	oo • nah eh • roop • theeyohn
	koo • tah • nee • ah
a sprain	**un esguince**
	oon ehs • geen • theh
some swelling	**una hinchazón**
	oo • nah een • chah • thohn
a stomachache	**dolor de estómago**
	doh • lohr deh ehs •
	toh • mah • goh
sunstroke	**una insolación**
	oo • nah ehn • soh • lah • theeyohn
I've been sick [ill] for…days.	**Llevo…días que me encuentro mal.**
	yeh • boh…dee • ahs keh meh
	ehn • kwehn • troh mahl

For Numbers, see page 20.

CONDITIONS

I'm…	**Soy…** *soy…*
anemic	**anémico** *m* /**anémica** *f*
	ah • neh • mee • koh/ah • neh • mee • kah

asthmatic	**asmático** *m*/**asmática** *f*
	ahs • mah • tee • koh/ahs • mah • tee • kah
diabetic	**diabético** *m*/**diabética** *f*
	deeyah • beh • tee • koh/
	deeyah • beh • tee • kah
epileptic	**epiléptico** *m*/**epileptica** *f*
	eh • pee • lehp • tee • koh/
	eh • pee • lehp • tee • kah
I'm allergic to antibiotics/penicillin.	**Soy alérgico** *m*/**alérgica** *f* **a los antibióticos/ la penicilina.**
	soy ah • lehr • khee • koh/
	ah • lehr • khee • kah ah lohs
	ahn • tee • beeyoh • tee • kohs/
	lah peh • nee • thee • lee • nah
I have...	**Tengo...** *tehn • goh*
arthritis	**artritis**
	ahr • tree • tees
(high/low) blood pressure.	**la tensión (alta/baja).**
	lah tehn • seeyohn (ahl • tah/bah • khah)
I have a heart condition.	**Padezco del corazón.**
	pah • dehth • koh dehl koh • rah • thon
I'm on...	**Estoy tomando...**
	ehs • toy toh • mahn • doh...

For Meals & Cooking, see page 169.

TREATMENT

Do I need a prescription/medicine?	**¿Necesito una receta/un medicamento?**
	neh • theh • see • toh oo • nah reh • theh •
	tah/oon meh • dee • kah • mehn • toh
Can you prescribe a generic drug? [unbranded medication]?	**¿Puede recetarme un medicamento genérico?**
	pweh • deh reh • theh • tahr • meh
	oon meh • dee • kah • mehn • toh
	kheh • neh • ree • koh

Where can I get it?	**¿Dónde puedo conseguirlo?**
	dohn • de pweh • doh kohn • seh • geer • loh

For What to Take, see page 150.

HOSPITAL

Notify my family, please.	**Por favor, avise a mi familia.**
	pohr fah • bohr ah • bee • seh ah mee
	fah • mee • leeyah
I'm in pain.	**Tengo dolor.**
	tehn • goh doh • lohr
I need a doctor/nurse.	**Necesito un médico/una enfermera.**
	neh • thee • see • toh oon meh • dee • koh/
	oo • nah ehn • fehr • meh • rah
When are visiting hours?	**¿Qué horas de visita tienen?**
	keh oh • rahs deh bee • see • tah
	teeyeh • nehn
I'm visiting…	**Vengo a hacer una visita a…**
	behn • goh ah ah • thehr oo • nah
	bee • see • tah ah…

DENTIST

I've broken a tooth/lost a filling.	**Se me ha roto un diente/ caído un empaste.**
	seh meh ah roh • toh oon deeyehn • teh/
	kah • ee • doh oon ehm • pahs • teh
I have a toothache.	**Tengo dolor de muelas.**
	tehn • goh doh • lohr deh mweh • lahs
Can you fix this denture?	**¿Puede arreglarme la dentadura postiza?**
	pweh • deh ah • rreh • glahr • meh
	lah dehn • tah • doo • rah pohs • tee • thah

GYNECOLOGIST

I have menstrual cramps/a vaginal infection.	**Tengo dolores menstruales/una infección vaginal.** _tehn • goh doh • loh • rehs_ _mehns • trwah • lehs/oo • nah_ _een • fehk • theeyohn bah • khee • nahl_
I missed my period.	**No me ha venido la regla.** _noh meh ah beh • nee • doh lah reh • glah_
I'm on the Pill.	**Tomo la píldora.** _toh • moh lah peel • doh • rah_
I'm (... months) pregnant.	**Estoy embarazada (de... meses).** _esh • toy ehm • bah • rah • thah • dah_ _(deh... meh • sehs)_
I'm not pregnant.	**No estoy embarazada.** _noh ehs • toy ehm • bah • rah • thah • dah_
My last period was...	**La última vez que me vino la regla fue...** _lah ool • tee • mah behth keh meh bee •_ _noh lah reh • glah fweh..._

OPTICIAN

I've lost...	**He perdido...** _eh pehr • dee • doh..._
a contact lens	**una lentilla** _oo • nah lehn • tee • yah_
my glasses	**las gafas** _lahs gah • fahs_
a lens	**una lente** _oo • nah lehn • teh_

PAYMENT & INSURANCE

How much?	**¿Cuánto es?** _kwahn • toh ehs_

Can I pay by credit card?	**¿Puedo pagar con tarjeta de crédito?**
	pweh • doh pah • _gahr_ kohn tahr • _kheh_ • tah deh _kreh_ • dee • toh
I have insurance.	**Tengo seguro médico.**
	tehn • goh seh • _goo_ • roh meh • dee • koh
I need a receipt for my insurance.	**Necesito una factura para el seguro médico.**
	neh • theh • _see_ • toh _oo_ • nah fahk • _too_ • rah _pah_ • rah ehl seh • _goo_ • roh _meh_ • dee • koh

PHARMACY

NEED TO KNOW

Where's the pharmacy?	**¿Dónde está la farmacia?** _dohn_ • deh ehs • _tah_ lah fahr • _mah_ • theeyah
What time does it open/close?	**¿A qué hora abre/cierra?** ah keh _oh_ • rah _ah_ • breh/theeyeh • rrah
What would you recommend for...?	**¿Qué me recomienda para...?** keh meh reh • koh • _meeyehn_ • dah _pah_ • rah...

How much do I take?	**¿Qué dosis me tomo?** keh <u>doh</u> • sees meh <u>toh</u> • moh
Can you fill [make up] this prescription?	**¿Puede darme este medicamento?** <u>pweh</u> • deh <u>dahr</u> • meh ehs • the meh • dee • kah • <u>mehn</u> • toh
I'm allergic to…	**Soy alérgico m/alérgica f a…** soy ah • <u>lehr</u> • khee • koh/ah • <u>lehr</u> • khee • kah ah…

WHAT TO TAKE

How much do I take?	**¿Qué dosis me tomo?** keh <u>doh</u> • sees meh <u>toh</u> • moh
How often?	**¿Con qué frecuencia?** kohn keh freh • <u>kwehn</u> • theeyah
Is it safe for children?	**¿Está indicado para niños?** ehs • <u>tah</u> een • dee • <u>kah</u> • doh pah • rah <u>nee</u> • nyohs
I'm taking…	**Estoy tomando…** ehs • <u>toy</u> toh • <u>mahn</u> • doh…
Are there side effects?	**¿Tiene algún efecto secundario?** teeyeh • neh ahl • <u>goon</u> eh • <u>fehk</u> • toh seh • koon • <u>dah</u> • reeyoh
I need something for…	**Necesito algo para…** neh • theh • <u>see</u> • toh ahl • goh pah • rah…
a cold	**el catarro** ehl kah • <u>tah</u> • rroh
a cough	**la tos** lah tohs
diarrhea	**la diarrea** lah deeyah • <u>rreh</u> • ah
a headache	**el dolor de cabeza** ehl doh • lohr deh kah • <u>beh</u> • thah
insect bites	**las picaduras de insecto** lahs pee • kah • <u>doo</u> • rahs

ⓘ

Pharmacies are easily identified by their green neon signs in the shape of a cross. Opening hours are generally from 9:00 a.m. until 1:30 p.m., closed for **siesta** in the afternoon and open from 4:30 p.m. until 8:00 p.m. There are 24-hour pharmacies available in larger cities. A list of pharmacies that are open at night or on weekends can be found in the windows of all pharmacies, and the list is also published in the local newspapers.

	deh een • sehk • toh
motion [travel]	**la cinetosis**
sickness	*lah thee • neh • toh • sees*
a sore throat	**las anginas**
	lahs ahn • khee • nahs
sunburn	**la quemadura solar**
	lah keh • mah • doo • rah soh • lahr

YOU MAY SEE... 👁

UNA VEZ/TRES VECES AL DÍA	once/three times a day
COMPRIMIDO	tablet
GOTA	drop
CUCHARADITA	teaspoon
DESPUÉS DE/ANTES DE/ CON LAS COMIDAS	after/ before/ with meals
CON EL ESTÓMAGO VACÍO	on an empty stomach
TRAGUE EL COMPRIMIDO ENTERO	swallow whole
PUEDE CAUSAR SOMNOLENCIA	may cause drowsiness
DE USO TÓPICO SOLAMENTE	for external use only

a toothache	**el dolor de muelas**
	ehl doh • lohr deh
	moo • eh • lahs
an upset stomach	**el malestar estomacal**
	ehl mah • lehs • tahr ehs • toh • mah • kahl

BASIC SUPPLIES

I'd like…	**Quiero…**
	keeyeh • roh…
acetaminophen	**paracetamol**
[paracetamol]	*pah • rah • thee • tah • mohl*
antiseptic cream	**crema antiséptica**
	kreh • mah ahn • tee • sehp • tee • kah
aspirin	**aspirinas**
	ahs • pee • ree • nahs
bandages	**tiritas**
	tee • ree • tahs
a comb	**un peine**
	oon peyee • neh
condoms	**preservativos**
	preh • sehr • bah • tee • bohs
contact lens	**líquido de lentillas**
	lee • kee • doh deh
solution	*lehn • tee • yahs*
deodorant	**desodorante**
	deh • soh • doh • rahn • teh
a hairbrush	**un cepillo de pelo**
	oon theh • pee • yoh deh peh • loh
hairspray	**laca**
	lah • kah
ibuprofen	**ibuprofeno**
	ee • boo • proh • feh • noh
insect repellent	**repelente de insectos**
	reh • peh • lehn • the deh een • sehk • tohs

lotion	**crema hidratante**	
	kreh • mah ee • drah • tahn • teh	
a nail file	**una lima de uñas**	
	oo • nah lee • mah deh oo • nyahs	
a (disposable) razor	**una cuchilla**	
	oo • nah koo • chee • yah	
razor blades	**hojas de afeitar**	
	oh • khahs deh ah • feyee • tahr	
sanitary napkins [towels]	**compresas**	
	kohm • preh • sahs	
shampoo/ conditioner	**champú/suavizante**	
	chahm • poo/swah • bee • thahn • teh	
soap	**jabón**	
	khah • bohn	
sunscreen	**protector solar**	
	proh • tehk • tohr soh • lahr	
tampons	**tampones**	
	tahm • poh • nehs	
tissues	**pañuelos de papel**	
	pah • nyweh • lohs deh pah • pehl	
toilet paper	**papel higiénico**	
	pah • pehl ee • kheeyeh • nee • koh	
a toothbrush	**un cepillo de dientes**	
	oon theh • pee • yoh deh deeyehn • tehs	
toothpaste	**pasta de dientes**	
	pahs • tah deh deeyehn • tehs	

CHILD HEALTH & EMERGENCY

Can you recommend a pediatrician?	**¿Puede recomendarme un pediatra?**
	pweh • deh reh • koh • mehn • dahr • meh oon peh • deeyah • trah
My child is allergic to…	**Mi hijo m/hija f es alérgico m/ alérgica f a…**
	mee ee • khoh/ee • khah ehs • alérgica f a…

ah • <u>lehr</u> • khee • koh/
ah • <u>lehr</u> • khee • kah ah…

My child is missing.	**Mi hijo m/hija f ha desaparecido.** mee <u>ee</u> • khoh/<u>ee</u> • khah ah deh • sah • pah • reh • <u>thee</u> • doh
Have you seen a boy/girl?	**¿Ha visto a un niño m/una niña f?** ah <u>bees</u> • toh ah oon nee • nyoh/<u>oo</u> • nah <u>nee</u> • nyah

For Baby Essentials, see page 134.

DISABLED TRAVELERS

ESSENTIAL

Is there…?	**¿Hay…?** aye…
access for the disabled	**acceso para los discapacitados** ahk • <u>theh</u> • soh <u>pah</u> • rah lohs dees • kah • pah • thee • <u>tah</u> • dohs
a wheelchair ramp	**una rampa para sillas de ruedas** <u>oo</u> • nah <u>rahm</u> • pah <u>pah</u> • rah see • yahs deh <u>rweh</u> • dahs
a disabled- accessible toilet	**un baño con acceso para discapacitados** oon <u>bah</u> • nyoh kohn ahk • <u>theh</u> • soh <u>pah</u> • rah dees • kah • pah • thee • <u>tah</u> • dohs
I need…	**Necesito…** neh • theh • <u>see</u> • toh…
assistance	**ayuda** ah • <u>yoo</u> • dah

an elevator [a lift]	**un ascensor**
	oon ahs • thehn • sohr
a ground-floor room	**una habitación en la planta baja**
	oo • nah ah • bee • tah • theeyohn
	ehn lah plahn • tah bah • khah

ASKING FOR ASSISTANCE

I'm disabled.	**Soy discapacitado** *m*/**discapacitada** *f*
	soy dees • kah • pah • thee • tah • doh/
	dees • kah • pah • thee • tah • dah
I'm deaf.	**Soy sordo** *m*/**sorda** *f*.
	soy sohr • doh/sohr • dah
I'm visually/hearing impaired.	**Tengo discapacidad visual/auditiva.**
	tehn • goh dees • kah • pah • thee • dahd
	bee • swahl/awoo • dee • tee • bah
I'm unable to walk far/use the stairs.	**No puedo caminar muy lejos/ subir las escaleras.**
	noh pweh • doh kah • mee • nahr mooy
	leh • khohs/soo • beer
	lahs ehs • kah • leh • rahs
Can I bring my wheelchair?	**¿Puedo traer la silla de ruedas?**
	pweh • doh trah • ehr lah see • yah deh
	rweh • dahs
Are guide dogs permitted?	**¿Permiten a perros guía?**
	pehr • mee • tehn ah peh • rrohs gee • ah
Can you help me?	**¿Puede ayudarme?**
	pweh • deh ah • yoo • dahr • meh
Please open/hold the door.	**Por favor, abra/aguante la puerta.**
	pohr fah • bohr ah • brah/
	ah • gwahn • teh lah pwehr • tah

FOOD & DRINK

EATING OUT

ESSENTIAL

Can you recommend a good restaurant/ bar?	**¿Puede recomendarme un buen restaurante/bar?**
	pweh • deh reh • koh • mehn • dahr • meh oon bwehn rehs • taw • rahn • teh/ bahr
Is there a traditional Spanish/an inexpensive restaurant nearby?	**¿Hay un restaurante típico español/ barato cerca de aquí?**
	aye oon rehs • taw • rahn • teh tee • pee • koh ehs • pah • nyohl/ bah • rah • toh thehr • kah deh ah • kee
A table for…, please.	**Una mesa para…, por favor.**
	oo • nah meh • sah pah • rah… pohr fah • bohr
Can we sit…?	**¿Podemos sentarnos…?**
	poh • deh • mohs sehn • tahr • nohs…
here/there	**aquí/allí**
	ah • kee/ah • yee
outside	**fuera** _fweh • rah_

in a non-smoking area	**en una zona de no fumadores**
	ehn oo • nah thoh • nah deh noh foo • mah • doh • rehs
I'm waiting for someone.	**Estoy esperando a alguien.**
	ehs • toy ehs • peh • rahn • doh ah ahl • geeyehn
Where are the toilets?	**¿Dónde están los servicios?**
	dohn • deh ehs • tahn lohs sehr • bee • theeyohs
A menu, please.	**Una carta, por favor.**
	oo • nah kahr • tah pohr fah • bohr
What do you recommend?	**¿Qué me recomienda?**
	keh meh reh • koh • meeyehn • dah
I'd like…	**Quiero…**
	keeyeh • roh…
Some more…, please.	**Quiero más…, por favor.**
	keeyeh • roh mahs… pohr fah • bohr
Enjoy your meal!	**¡Que aproveche!**
	keh ah • proh • beh • cheh
The check [bill], please.	**La cuenta, por favor.**
	lah kwen • tah pohr fah • bohr
Is service included?	**¿Está incluido el servicio?**
	ehs • tah een • kloo • ee • doh ehl sehr • bee • theeyoh
Can I pay by credit card?	**¿Puedo pagar con tarjeta de crédito?**
	pweh • doh pah • gahr kohn tahr • kheh • tah deh kreh • dee • toh
Can I have a receipt?	**¿Podría darme un recibo?**
	poh • dree • ah dahr • meh oon reh • thee • boh
Thank you!	**¡Gracias!**
	grah • theeyahs

WHERE TO EAT

Can you recommend...?	**¿Puede recomendarme...?** _pweh • deh reh • koh • mehn • dahr • meh..._
a restaurant	**un restaurante** _oon rehs • taw • rahn • teh_
a bar	**un bar** _oon bahr_
a cafe	**un café** _oon kah • feh_
a fast-food place	**un restaurante de comida rápida** _oon rehs • taw • rahn • teh deh koh • mee • dah rah • pee • dah_
a tapas bar	**un bar de tapas** _oon bahr deh tah • pahs_
a cheap restaurant	**un restaurante barato** _oon rehs • taw • rahn • teh bah • rah • toh_
an expensive restaurant	**un restaurante caro** _oon rehs • taw • rahn • teh kah • roh_
a restaurant with a good view	**un restaurante con buenas vistas** _oon rehs • taw • rahn • teh kohn bweh • nash bees • tahs_
an authentic/ a non-touristy restaurant	**un restaurante auténtico/no turístico** _oon rehs • taw • rahn • teh awtehn • tee • koh/noh too • reesh • tee • koh_

RESERVATIONS & PREFERENCES

I'd like to reserve a table...	**Quiero reservar una mesa...** _keeyeh • roh reh • sehr • bahr oo • nah meh • sah..._
for two	**para dos** _pah • rah dohs_
for this evening	**para esta noche** _pah • rah ehs • tah noh • cheh_

YOU MAY HEAR...

¿Tiene reserva?	Do you have
teeyeh • neh reh • sehr • bah	a reservation?
¿Cuántos son?	How many?
kwahn • tohs sohn	
¿Fumador o no fumador?	Smoking or
foo • mah • dohr oh noh foo • mah • dohr	non-smoking?
¿Está listo m/lista f para pedir?	Are you ready
ehs • tah lees • toh/lees • tah pah • rah	to order?
peh • deer	
¿Qué va a tomar?	What would
keh bah ah toh • mahr	you like?
Le recomiendo...	I recommend...
leh reh • koh • meeyehn • doh...	
Que aproveche.	Enjoy your meal.
keh ah • proh • beh • cheh	

for tomorrow at...	**para mañana a la/las...**
	pah • rah mah • nyah • nah ah lah/lahs...
A table for two, please.	**Una mesa para dos, por favor.**
	oo • nah meh • sah pah • rah dohs
	pohr fah • bohr
We have a reservation.	**Tenemos una reserva.**
	teh • neh • mohs oo • nah reh • sehr • bah
My name is...	**Me llamo...**
	meh yah • moh...
Can we sit...?	**¿Podríamos sentarnos...?**
	poh • dree • ah • mohs sehn • tahr • nohs...
here/there	**aquí/allí**
	ah • kee/ah • yee
outside	**fuera**
	fweh • rah

in a non-smoking area	**en una zona de no fumadores**
	ehn <u>oo</u> • nah <u>thoh</u> • nah deh noh
	foo • mah • <u>doh</u> • rehs
by the window	**al lado de la ventana**
	ahl <u>lah</u> • doh de lah behn • <u>tah</u> • nah
in the shade/sun	**¿Me puede dar una mesa a la sombra/**
	al sol?
	meh <u>pweh</u> • deh dahr <u>oo</u> • nah
	<u>meh</u> • sah ah lah <u>sohm</u> • brah/ahl sohl
Where are the toilets?	**¿Dónde están los servicios?**
	<u>dohn</u> • deh ehs • <u>tahn</u>
	lohs sehr • <u>bee</u> • theeyohs

For Grammar, see page 12.

HOW TO ORDER

Waiter/Waitress!	**¡Camarero m/Camarera f!**
	kah • mah • <u>reh</u> • roh/kah • mah • <u>reh</u> • rah
We're ready to order.	**Estamos listos para pedir.**
	ehs • <u>tah</u> • mohs <u>lees</u> • tohs
	pah • rah peh • <u>deer</u>
May I see the wine list?	**La carta de vinos, por favor.**
	lah <u>kahr</u> • tah deh <u>bee</u> • nohs pohr fah • <u>bohr</u>
I'd like…	**Quiero…** *<u>keeyeh</u> • roh…*

a bottle of…	**una botella de…**
	_oo_ • nah boh • _teh_ • yah deh…
a carafe of…	**una garrafa de…**
	_oo_ • nah gah • _rrah_ • fah deh…
a glass of…	**un vaso de…**
	oon _bah_ • soh deh…
Can I have a menu?	**La carta, por favor.**
	lah _kahr_ • tah pohr fah • _bohr_
Do you have…?	**¿Tiene…?**
	teeyeh • neh…
a menu in English	**una carta en inglés**
	_oo_ • nah _kahr_ • tah ehn een • _glehs_
a fixed-price menu	**el menú del día**
	ehl meh • _noo_ dehl _dee_ • ah
a children's menu	**una carta para niños**
	_oo_ • nah _kahr_ • tah _pah_ • rah _nee_ • nyohs
What do you recommend?	**¿Qué me recomienda?**
	keh meh reh • koh • _meeyehn_ • dah
What's this?	**¿Qué es esto?**
	keh ehs _ehs_ • toh
What's in it?	**¿Qué lleva?**
	keh _yeh_ • bah
Is it spicy?	**¿Es picante?**
	ehs pee • _kahn_ • teh
I'd like…	**Quiero…** _keeyeh_ • roh…
More…, please.	**Más…, por favor.**
	mahs…pohr fah • _bohr_
With/Without…	**Con/Sin…**
	kohn/seen…
I can't have…	**No puedo tomar…**
	noh _pweh_ • doh toh • _mahr_…
rare	**muy poco hecho** m/**hecha** f
	mooy _poh_ • koh eh • choh/eh • chah
medium	**medio hecho** m/**hecha** f
	meh • deeyoh eh • choh/eh • chah

well-done	**bien hecho** m/**hecha** f
	beeyehn eh•choh/eh•chah
It's to go [take away].	**Es para llevar.**
	ehs pah•rah yeh•bahr

For Drinks, see page 192.

COOKING METHODS

baked	**al horno**
	ahl ohr•noh
boiled	**hervido** m/**hervida** f
	ehr•bee•doh/ehr•bee•da
braised	**a fuego lento**
	ah fweh•goh lehn•toh
breaded	**empanado** m/**empanada** f
	ehm•pah•nah•doh/ehm•pah•nah•dah
creamed	**con nata**
	kohn nah•tah
diced	**cortado en taquitos**
	kohr•tah•doh ehn tah•kee•tohs
fileted	**cortado en filetes**
	kohr•tah•doh ehn fee•leh•tehs
fried	**frito** m/**frita** f
	free•toh/free•tah
grilled	**a la plancha**
	ah lah plahn•chah

poached	**escalfado** m/**escalfada** f
	ehs • kahl • <u>fah</u> • doh/ehs • kahl • <u>fah</u> • dah
roasted	**asado** m/**asada** f
	ah • <u>sah</u> • doh/ah • <u>sah</u> • dah
sautéed	**salteado** m/**salteada** f
	sahl • teh • <u>ah</u> • doh/sahl • teh • <u>ah</u> • dah
smoked	**ahumado** m/**ahumada** f
	ah • oo • <u>mah</u> • doh/ah • oo • <u>mah</u> • dah
steamed	**al vapor**
	ahl bah • <u>pohr</u>
stewed	**guisado** m/**guisada** f
	gee • <u>sah</u> • doh/gee • <u>sah</u> • dah
stuffed	**relleno** m/**rellena** f
	reh • <u>yeh</u> • noh/reh • <u>yeh</u> • nah

DIETARY REQUIREMENTS

I'm…	**Soy…**
	soy…
diabetic	**diabético** m/**diabética** f
	dee • ah • <u>beh</u> • tee • koh/
	dee • ah • <u>beh</u> • tee • kah
lactose intolerant	**alérgico** m/**alérgica** f **a la lactosa**
	ah • <u>lehr</u> • khee • koh/ah • <u>lehr</u> • khee •
	kah ah lah lahk • <u>toh</u> • sah
vegetarian	**vegetariano** m/**vegetariana** f
	beh • kheh • tah • <u>reeyah</u> • noh/beh • kheh •
	tah • <u>reeyah</u> • nah
I'm allergic to…	**Soy alérgico** m/**alérgica** f **a…**
	soy ah • <u>lehr</u> • khee • koh/ah • <u>lehr</u> • khee •
	kah ah…
I can't eat…	**No puedo comer…**
	noh <u>pweh</u> • doh koh • <u>mehr</u>…
dairy products	**productos lácteos**
	proh • <u>dook</u> • tohs lahk • teh • ohs

gluten	**gluten**
	gloo • tehn
nuts	**frutos secos**
	froo • tohs seh • kohs
pork	**carne de cerdo**
	kahr • neh deh thehr • doh
shellfish	**marisco**
	mah • rees • koh
spicy foods	**comidas picantes**
	koh • mee • dahs pee • kahn • tehs
wheat	**trigo**
	tree • goh
Is it halal/kosher?	**¿Es halal/kosher?**
	ehs ah • lahl/koh • sehr
Do you have...?	**¿Tiene...?**
	teeyeh • neh
skimmed milk	**leche desnatada**
	leh • cheh dehs • nah • tah • dah
whole milk	**leche entera**
	leh • cheh ehn • teh • rah
soya milk	**leche de soja**
	leh • cheh deh soh • khah

DINING WITH CHILDREN

Do you have children's portions?	**¿Sirven raciones para niños?**
	seer • behn rah • theeyoh • nehs pah • rah nee • nyohs
Can I have a highchair/child's seat?	**Una trona/silla para niños, por favor.**
	oo • nah troh • nah/see • yah pah • rah nee • nyohs pohr fah • bohr
Where can I feed/change the baby?	**¿Dónde puedo darle de comer/cambiar al niño?**
	dohn • deh pweh • doh dahr • leh deh koh • mehr/kahm • beeyahr ahl nee • nyoh

Can you warm this?	**¿Puede calentar esto?**
	pweh • deh kah • lehn • tahr ehs • toh

For Traveling with Children, see page 132.

HOW TO COMPLAIN

When will our food be ready?	**¿Cuánto más tardará la comida?**
	kwahn • toh mahs tahr • dah • rah lah koh • mee • dah
We can't wait any longer.	**No podemos esperar más.**
	noh poh • deh • mohs ehs • peh • rahr mahs
We're leaving.	**Nos vamos.**
	nohs bah • mohs
I didn't order this.	**Esto no es lo que pedí.**
	ehs • toh noh ehs loh keh peh • dee
I ordered…	**Pedí…**
	peh • dee…
I can't eat this.	**No puedo comerme esto.**
	noh pweh • doh koh • mehr • meh ehs • toh
This is too…	**Esto está demasiado…**
	ehs • toh ehs • ta deh • mah • seeyah • doh…
cold/hot	**frío/caliente**
	free • oh/kah • leeyehn • teh
salty/spicy	**salado/picante**
	sah • lah • doh/pee • kahn • teh

Restaurants are generally required to include service charges as part of the bill, so tipping isn't customary. If you wish to leave a tip for good service, just round up the bill to the nearest euro or two.

tough/bland	**duro/soso**
	doo • roh/soh • soh
This isn't clean/ fresh.	**Esto no está limpio/fresco.**
	ehs • toh noh ehs • tah leem • peeyoh/ frehs • koh

PAYING

The check [bill], please.	**La cuenta, por favor.**
	lah kwehn • tah pohr fah • bohr
Separate checks [bills], please.	**Cuentas separadas, por favor.**
	kwehn • tahs seh • pah • rah • dahs pohr fah • bohr
It's all together.	**Póngalo todo junto.**
	pohn • gah • loh toh • doh khoon • toh
Is service included?	**¿Está incluido el servicio?**
	ehs • tah een • kloo • ee • doh ehl sehr • bee • theeyoh
What's this amount for?	**¿De qué es esta cantidad?**
	deh keh ehs ehs • tah kahn • tee • dahth
I didn't have that. I had…	**Yo no tomé eso. Tomé…**
	yoh noh toh • meh eh • soh toh • meh…
Can I pay by credit card?	**¿Puedo pagar con tarjeta de crédito?**
	pweh • doh pah • gahr kohn tahr • kheh • tah deh kreh • dee • toh
Can I have a receipt/ an itemized bill?	**¿Podría darme un recibo/una cuenta detallada?**
	poh • dree • ah dahr • meh oon

reh • thee • boh/oo • nah kwehn • tah deh •
tah • yah • dah

That was delicious! **¡Estuvo delicioso!**
ehs • too • boh deh • lee • theeyoh • soh

I've already paid. **Ya he pagado**
yah eh pah • gah • doh

MEALS & COOKING

BREAKFAST

el agua	water
ehl ah • gwah	
el café/el té...	coffee/tea...
ehl kah • feh/ehl teh...	
con azúcar	with sugar
kohn ah • thoo • kahr	
con edulcorante artificial	with artificial
kohn eh • dool • koh • rahn • teh	sweetener
ahr • tee • fee • theeyahl	
con leche	with milk
kohn leh • cheh	
descafeinado	decaf
dehs • kah • feyee • nah • doh	

(i)

El desayuno (breakfast) is usually served from
8:00 a.m. to 10:00 a.m. **La comida** (lunch), generally
the largest meal of the day, is served from 2:00-4:00 p.m.
La cena (dinner) is typically smaller and lighter than in
the U.S. or U.K., and is usually served after 9:00 p.m. For
a snack between meals, you can get **tapas** in smaller
restaurants and some bars.

solo	black
soh • loh	
los cereales (calientes/fríos)	(cold/hot) cereal
lohs theh • reh • ah • lehs	
(kah • leeyehn • tehs/free • ohs)	
los fiambres	cold cuts
lohs fee • ahm • brehs	[charcuterie]
la harina de avena	oatmeal
lah ah • ree • nah deh ah • beh • nah	
el huevo…	egg…
ehl weh • boh…	
duro/pasado por agua	hard-/soft-boiled
doo • roh/pah • sah • doh pohr ah • gwah	
frito	fried
free • toh	
revuelto	scrambled
reh • bwehl • toh	
los huevos a la flamenca	baked eggs with
lohs weh • bohs ah lah flah • mehn • kah	tomato, onion
	and ham
la leche	milk
lah leh • cheh	
la magdalena	muffin
lah mahg • dah • leh • nah	
la mantequilla	butter
lah mahn • teh • kee • yah	
la mermelada/la jalea	jam/jelly
lah mehr • meh • lah • dah/khah • leh • ah	
el muesli	granola [muesli]
ehl mwehs • lee	
el pan	bread
ehl pahn	
el panecillo	roll
ehl pah • neh • thee • yoh	
el queso	cheese

ehl keh • soh
la salchicha   sausage
lah sahl • chee • chah
el tocino   bacon
ehl toh • thee • noh
la tortilla...   omelet...
lah tohr • tee • yah...
  de patatas   with potato (and
  deh pah • tah • tahs   sometimes onion)
  de jamón   with ham
  deh khah • mohn
  paisana   with potatoes,
  payee • sah • nah   peas and shrimp
                                or ham
  de queso   with cheese
  deh keh • soh
  de setas   with mushrooms
  deh seh • tahs
la tostada   toast
lah tohs • tah • dah
el yogur   yogurt
ehl yoh • goor
el zumo de...   ...juice
ehl thoo • moh deh...

manzana   apple
mahn • thah • nah

pomelo   grapefruit
poh • meh • loh

naranja   orange
nah • rahn • khah

APPETIZERS

las aceitunas (rellenas)   (stuffed) olives
lahs ah • theyee • too • nahs (reh • yeh • nahs)

las albóndigas   meatballs
lahs ahl • bohn • dee • gahs

el bacalao   dried salt cod
ehl bah • kah • laoh

los boquerones en vinagre   anchovies marinated
lohs boh • keh • roh • nehs ehn bee •   in garlic and
nah • greh   olive oil

los callos   tripe in hot paprika
lohs kah • yohs   sauce

los caracoles   snails
lohs kah • rah • koh • lehs

los champiñones al ajillo   mushrooms fried in
lohs chahm • pee • nyoh • nehs ahl ah •   olive oil
khee • yoh   with garlic

las croquetas   croquettes
lahs kroh • keh • tahs   with various fillings

las gambas al ajillo   broiled shrimp in
lahs gahm • bahs ahl ah • khee • yoh   garlic

Tapas are small bites to eat or snacks, served in cafés and bars. **Una tapa** is a mouthful, **una ración** is a half plate and **una porción** is a generous serving.

el pan con tomate
ehl pahn kohn toh • mah • teh
toasted bread with garlic, tomato and olive oil

los pescados fritos
lohs pehs • kah • dohs free • tohs
fried fish

los pimientos
lohs pee • meeyehn • tohs
peppers

los pinchos
lohs peen • chohs
grilled, skewered meat

los quesos
lohs keh • sohs
cheese platter

la tortilla española
lah tohr • tee • yah ehs • pah • nyoh • lah
potato omelet

SOUP

el caldo gallego
ehl kahl • doh gah • yeh • goh
stew of cabbage, potatoes, beans and meat, from Galicia region

el cocido
ehl koh • thee • doh
chickpea stew with potatoes, cabbage, turnips, beef, bacon, chorizo and black pudding

el consomé al jerez
ehl kohn • soh • meh ahl kheh • rehth
chicken broth with sherry

la fabada asturiana
lah fah • bah • dah ahs • too • reeyah • nah
white bean stew

el gazpacho
ehl gahth • pah • choh
cold tomato soup

el marmitako
ehl mahr • mee • tah • koh
tuna fish and potato stew, from the Basque region

la sopa... *lah soh • pah...*
...soup

castellana
kahs • teh • yah • nah

soup with garlic, chunks of ham and a poached egg

de ajo blanco
deh ah • khoh blahn • koh

soup with garlic and almond, served cold, popular in Andalucia

de habas
deh ah • bahs

bean soup

de mariscos
deh mah • rees • kohs

seafood soup

de pollo
deh poh • yoh

chicken soup

de tomate
deh toh • mah • teh

tomato soup

de verduras
deh behr • doo • rahs

vegetable soup

FISH & SEAFOOD

la almeja
lah ahl • meh • khah

clam

el arenque
ehl ah • rehn • keh

herring

el atún
ehl ah • toon

tuna

el bacalao a la vizcaína
ehl bah • kah • laoh ah lah

cod with dried peppers and onions

el bacalao
ehl bah • kah • laoh

cod

el besugo
ehl beh • soo • goh

sea bream

el boquerón
ehl boh • keh • rohn

fresh baby anchovy

la caballa
lah kah • bah • yah

mackerel

el calamar
ehl kah•lah•mahr

squid

los calamares a la romana
lohs kah•lah•mahr•ehs ah lah roh•mah•nah

deep-fried battered squid

el cangrejo
ehl kahn•greh•khoh

crab

el chipirón
ehl chee•pee•rohn

small whole squid

las cigalas
lahs thee•gah•lahs

crayfish

las cigalas cocidas
lahs thee•gah•lahs koh•thee•dahs

boiled crayfish

el fletán
ehl fleh•tahn

halibut

la gamba
lah gahm•bah

shrimp

las gambas en cerveza
lahs gahm•bahs ehn thehr•beh•thah

shrimp in beer

la langosta
lah lahn•gohs•tah

lobster

el lenguado
ehl lehn•gwah•doh

sole

la lubina *lah loo • bee • nah*	sea bass
la mariscada *lah mah • rees • kah • dah*	cold mixed shellfish
los mejillones *lohs meh • khee • yoh • nehs*	mussels
los mejillones en escabeche *lohs meh • khee • yohn • ehs ehn* *ehs • kah • beh • cheh*	mussels in a marinade
la merluza *lah mehr • loo • thah*	hake
la merluza a la sidra *lah mehr • loo • thah ah lah see • drah*	hake in cider
el mero *ehl meh • roh*	grouper
la ostra *lah ohs • trah*	oyster
el pez espada *ehl pehth ehs • pah • dah*	swordfish
el pulpo *ehl pool • poh*	octopus
el pulpo a la gallega *ehl pool • poh ah lah gah • yeh • gah*	octopus with olive oil and paprika
el salmón *ehl sahl • mohn*	salmon
el tiburón *ehl tee • boo • rohn*	shark
la trucha *lah troo • chah*	trout
la trucha a la navarra *lah troo • chah ah lah nah • bah • rrah*	grilled trout stuffed with ham
la zarzuela de pescado *lah thahr • thweh • lah* *deh pehs • kah • doh*	mixed fish and sea- food cooked in broth, served over bread

MEAT & POULTRY

la asadurilla de cordero
lah ah•sah•doo•rree•yah deh kohr•deh•roh
lamb's liver

la butifarra
lah boo•tee•fah•rrah
spiced pork sausage, popular in Cataluña and Valencia

los callos a la madrileña
lohs kah•yohs ah lah mah•dree•leh•nyah
tripe stew, a Madrid specialty

la carne
lah kahr•neh
meat

la carne de cerdo
lah kahr•neh deh thehr•doh
pork

la carne picada
lah kahr•neh pee•kah•dah
ground beef

la carne de vaca
lah kahr•neh deh bah•kah
beef

el chorizo
ehl choh•ree•thoh
highly-seasoned, red, pork sausage common in paellas and on pizzas

la chuleta
lah choo•leh•tah
chop

el cochifrito navarro
ehl koh•chee•free•toh nah•bah•rroh
deep-fried lamb pieces

el conejo
ehl koh•neh•khoh
rabbit

el cordero
ehl kohr•deh•roh
lamb

la cordorniz
lah kohr•dohr•neeth
quail

las costillas de cerdo
lahs kohs•tee•yahs deh thehr•doh
pork ribs

las empanadas
lahs ehm • pah • nah • dahs

pastry filled with meat, chicken or tuna, a specialty of Galicia

los espárragos montañeses
lohs ehs • pah • rrah • gohs mohn • tah • nyeh • sehs

calves's tails

la falda de buey
lah fahl • dah deh bwehy

beef flank steak

el filete
ehl fee • leh • teh

steak

las gallinejas
lahs gah • yee • neh • khahs

fried lamb intestine

el guisado de riñones
ehl gee • sah • doh deh ree • nyoh • nehs

kidney stew

el hígado
ehl ee • gah • doh

liver

el jamón
ehl khah • mohn

ham

el jamón ibérico
ehl khah • mohn ee • beh • ree • koh

aged Iberian ham

el jamón serrano
ehl khah • mohn seh • rrah • noh

dry-cured serrano ham

el lacón con grelos
ehl lah • kohn kohn greh • lohs

salted ham with turnip greens, typical of Galicia

las magras con tomate
lahs mah • grahs kohn toh • mah • teh

lightly fried ham dipped in tomato sauce

las manos de cerdo
lahs mah • nohs deh thehr • doh

pig's feet [trotters]

las mollejas de ternera
lahs moh • yeh • khahs deh tehr • neh • rah

veal sweetbread

la morcilla
lah mohr • thee • yah

blood sausage

la paella...
lah pah • eh • yah...

    de carne
    deh kahr • neh

    de marisco
    deh mah • rees • koh

    de verduras
    deh behr • doo • rahs

    valenciana
    bah • lehn • theeyah • nah

    zamorana
    thah • moh • rah • nah

paella...

    with chicken and sausage (may be made with beef)

    with seafood

    with vegetables

    with chicken, shrimp, mussels, squid, peas, tomato, garlic, olive oil, paprika; from the Valencia region

    with ham, pork loin, pig's feet

Paella is a specialty dish of Spain. Traditional **paella**, which originated in Valencia, includes rice, saffron, vegetables, rabbit and chicken. **Paella de marisco** (seafood **paella**) is a very popular version of this dish, especially along the coast. Other delicious versions are noted above.

las patatas con chorizo *lahs pah • tah • tahs kohn choh • ree • thoh*	potatoes with chorizo
el pato *ehl pah • toh*	duck
el pavo *ehl pah • boh*	turkey
el pollo *ehl poh • yoh*	chicken
el pollo frito *ehl poh • yoh free • toh*	fried chicken
el riñón *ehl ree • nyohn*	kidney
la salchicha *lah sahl • chee • chah*	sausage
el salchichón *ehl sahl • chee • chohn*	salami-type sausage
el solomillo *ehl soh • loh • mee • yoh*	filet mignon
la ternera *lah tehr • neh • rah*	veal
el tocino *ehl toh • thee • noh*	bacon
la trucha a la navarra *lah troo • chah ah lah nah • bah • rrah*	trout fried with a piece of ham
el venado *ehl beh • nah • doh*	venison

VEGETABLES & STAPLES

la aceituna *lah ah • theyee • too • nah*	olive
la acelga *lah ah • thehl • gah*	chard
el aguacate *ehl ah • gwah • khah • teh*	avocado

el ajo
ehl ah • khoh

garlic

la albahaca
lah ahl • bah • ah • kah

basil

la alcachofa (salteada)
lah ahl • kah • choh • fah (sahl • teh • ah • dah)

(sauteed) artichoke

la alcaparra
lah ahl • kah • pah • rrah

caper

el anís
ehl ah • nees

aniseed

el apio
ehl ah • peeyoh

celery

el arroz...
ehl ah • rrohth...

rice...

   con habas y nabos
   kohn ah • bahs ee nah • bohs

with beans
and turnips

   a la cubana
   ah lah koo • bah • nah

with fried eggs and
banana fritters

   empedrado
   ehm • peh • drah • doh

with tomatoes
and cod and a top
layer of white beans

   santanderino
   sahn • tahn • deh • ree • noh

with salmon and milk

el azafrán
ehl ah • thah • frahn

saffron

los bajoques farcides
lohs bah • khoh • kehs fahr • thee • dehs

red peppers stuffed
with rice, pork
and tomatoes;
from Catalonia

la batata *lah bah • tah • tah*

yam

la berenjena
lah beh • rehn • kheh • nah

eggplant [aubergine]

el brécol
ehl breh • kohl

broccoli

los brotes de soja
lohs broh•tehs deh soh•khah
bean sprouts

el calabacín
ehl kah•lah•bah•theen
zucchini [courgette]

la cassolada
lah kahs•soh•lah•dah
rice casserole with thrushes (small birds) and ribs, from Catalonia

la cebolla
lah theh•boh•yah
onion

el champiñon (a la plancha/salteado)
ehl chahm•pee•nyohn (ah lah plahn•chah/sahl•teh•ah•doh)
(grilled/sautéed) mushroom

la coliflor
lah koh•lee•flohr
cauliflower

el espárrago
ehl ehs•pah•rrah•goh
asparagus

la espinaca
lah ehs•pee•nah•kah
spinach

la faba
lah fah•bah
white bean

el guisante
ehl gee•sahn•teh
pea

las habas a la catalana
lahs ah•bahs a lah kah•tah•lah•nah
broad bean

la harina
lah ah•ree•nah
flour

la judía
lah khoo•dee•ah
bean

la judía verde
lah khoo•dee•ah behr•deh
green bean

la lechuga
lah leh•choo•gah
lettuce

la lenteja
lah lehn•teh•khah
lentil

el maíz
ehl mah • eeth

corn

la menestra
lah meh • nehs • trah

vegetable stew

las migas de pastor
lahs mee • gahs deh pahs • tohr

bread fried with bacon and dried peppers

el pan
ehl pahn

bread

la pasta
lah pahs • tah

pasta

la patata
lah pah • tah • tah

potato

el pepino
ehl peh • pee • noh

cucumber

el perejil
ehl peh • reh • kheel

parsley

el pimiento relleno
ehl pee • meeyehn • toh reh • yeh • noh

stuffed pepper

el pimiento rojo/verde
ehl pee • meeyehn • toh roh • khoh/ behr • deh

red/green pepper

el repollo
ehl reh • poh • yoh

cabbage

la seta
lah seh • tah

mushroom

el tomate
ehl toh • mah • teh

tomato

la verdura
lah behr • doo • rah

vegetable

la zanahoria
lah thah • nah • oh • reeyah

carrot

FRUIT

el albaricoque *ehl ahl•bah•ree•<u>koh</u>•keh*	apricot
el arándano *ehl ah•<u>rahn</u>•dah•noh*	blueberry
el arándano rojo *ehl ah•<u>rahn</u>•dah•noh <u>roh</u>•khoh*	cranberry
la cereza *lah theh•<u>reh</u>•thah*	cherry
la ciruela *lah thee•<u>rweh</u>•lah*	plum
el coco *ehl <u>koh</u>•koh*	coconut
la frambuesa *lah frahm•<u>bweh</u>•sah*	raspberry
la fresa *lah <u>freh</u>•sah*	strawberry
la fruta *lah <u>froo</u>•tah*	fruit
la guayaba *lah gwah•<u>yah</u>•bah*	guava
el kiwi *ehl <u>kee</u>•wee*	kiwi
la lima *lah <u>lee</u>•mah*	lime
el limón *ehl lee•<u>mohn</u>*	lemon
la mandarina *lah mahn•dah•<u>ree</u>•nah*	tangerine
el mango *ehl <u>mahn</u>•goh*	mango
la manzana *lah mahn•<u>thah</u>•nah*	apple
el melocotón	peach

ehl meh • loh • koh • tohn
el melón melon

ehl meh • lohn
la naranja orange

lah nah • rahn • khah
la papaya papaya

lah pah • pah • yah
la pera pear

lah peh • rah
la piña pineapple

lah pee • nyah
el plátano banana

ehl plah • tah • noh
el pomelo grapefruit

ehl poh • meh • loh
la sandía watermelon

lah sahn • dee • ah
la uva grape

lah oo • bah

CHEESE

el queso... ...cheese
ehl keh • soh...

blando
blahn • doh

soft, mild-flavored

de Burgos
deh boor • gohs

soft, creamy
regional variety

Cabrales
kah • brah • lehs

tangy, blue-veined
regional variety

cremoso
kreh • moh • soh

cream

curado
koo • rah • doh

ripe

de leche de cabra
deh leh • cheh deh kah • brah

from goat's milk

duro
doo • roh

hard

fuerte
fwehr • teh

strong

Manchego
mahn • cheh • goh

hard cheese from
Manchego sheep's
milk

Perilla
peh • ree • yah

firm, bland
regional variety

rallado
rah • yah • doh

grated

requesón
reh • keh • sohn

cottage

Roncal
rohn • kahl

sharp goat cheese,
salted and smoked,
regional variety

suave
swah • beh

mild

tipo roquefort
tee • poh roh • qeh • fohrt

blue

DESSERT

el arroz con leche rice pudding
ehl ah • rroth kohn leh • cheh

el brazo de gitano sponge cake roll with
ehl brah • thoh deh khee • tah • noh cream filling

el buñuelo thin, deep-fried
ehl boo • nyweh • loh fritter, covered
in sugar

el canutillo custard pastry horn
ehl kah • noo • tee • yoh with cinnamon

el churro deep-fried fritter
ehl choo • rroh sprinkled with sugar

la filloa crepe (used in sweet
lah fee • yoh • ah or savory dishes),
typical of Galicia
region

el flan caramel custard
ehl flahn

la galleta cookie [biscuit]
lah gah • yeh • tah

el helado ice cream
ehl eh • lah • doh

la leche frita fried milk custard
lah leh • cheh free • tah

la mantecada *lah mahn • teh • kah • dah* small sponge cake

la manzana asada baked apple
lah mahn • thah • nah ah • sah • dah

el pastel de queso cheesecake
ehl pahs • tehl deh keh • soh

el sorbete sorbet
ehl sohr • beh • teh

la tarta de Santiago dense almond
lah tahr • tah deh sahn • teeyah • goh cake topped
with powdered sugar

el tocino de cielo	egg yolk custard
ehl toh • thee • noh deh theeyeh • loh	

SAUCES & CONDIMENTS

salt	**la sal**
	lah sahl
black pepper	**la pimienta negra**
	lah pee • meeyehn • tah neh • grah
mustard	**mostaza**
	mohs • tah • thah
ketchup	**ketchup**
	keht • choop
sugar	**el azúcar**
	ehl ah • thoo • kahr

AT THE MARKET

Where are the carts [trolleys]/baskets?	**¿Dónde están los carritos/las cestas?**
	dohn • deh ehs • tahn lohs kah • rree • tohs/ lahs thehs • tahs
Where is …?	**¿Donde está…?**
	dohn • deh ehs • tah…
I'd like some of that/this.	**Quiero un poco de eso/esto.**
	keeyeh • roh oon poh • koh deh eh • soh/ ehs • toh
Can I taste it?	**¿Puedo probarlo?**
	pweh • doh proh • bahr • loh
I'd like…	**Quiero…**
	keeyeh • roh…
a kilo/half-kilo of…	**un kilo/medio kilo de…**
	oon kee • loh/meh • deeyoh kee • loh deh…
a liter of…	**un litro de…**
	oon lee • troh deh…
a piece of…	**un trozo de…**

YOU MAY HEAR...

¿Necesita ayuda?	Can I help you?
neh • theh • <u>see</u> • tah ah • <u>yoo</u> • dah	
¿Qué desea?	What would you
keh deh • seh • ah	like?
¿Algo más?	Anything else?
<u>ahl</u> • goh mahs	
Son...euros.	That's...euros.
sohn...<u>ew</u> • rohs	

In Spain, food is often purchased at local family-run markets. These are excellent places for regional and specialty foods, fresh fruit and vegetables, meat and baked goods. **Hipermercados** (large grocery store chains) are also common, but these are usually found on the outskirts of town or in the suburbs. These stores have a larger selection than regular supermarkets, and are often less expensive. **Alcampo**, **Carrefour** and **Hipercor** are common chains. **El Corte Inglés** is a popular department store chain that has a supermarket on the ground floor in some locations.

	oon <u>troh</u> • thoh deh...
a slice of...	**una rodaja de...**
	<u>oo</u> • nah roh • <u>dah</u> khah deh...
More/Less.	**Más/Menos.**
	mahs/<u>meh</u> • nohs
How much?	**¿Cuánto es?**
	<u>kwahn</u> • toh ehs
Where do I pay?	**¿Dónde se paga?**
	<u>dohn</u> • deh seh <u>pah</u> • gah

A bag, please.	**Una bolsa, por favor.**
	oo • nah <u>bohl</u> • sah pohr fah • <u>bohr</u>
I'm being helped.	**Ya me atienden.**
	yah meh ah • <u>teeyehn</u> • dehn

IN THE KITCHEN

bottle opener	**el abrebotellas**
	ehl ah • breh • boh • <u>teh</u> • yahs
bowl	**el cuenco**
	ehl <u>kwehn</u> • koh
can opener	**el abrelatas**
	ehl ah • breh • <u>lah</u> • tahs
corkscrew	**el sacacorchos**
	ehl sah • kah • <u>kohr</u> • chohs
cup	**la taza**
	lah <u>tah</u> • thah
fork	**el tenedor**
	ehl teh • neh • <u>dohr</u>
frying pan	**la sartén**
	lah sahr • <u>tehn</u>
glass	**el vaso**
	ehl <u>bah</u> • soh
(steak) knife	**el cuchillo (de carne)**
	ehl koo • <u>chee</u> • yoh (deh <u>kahr</u> • neh)

Measurements in Europe are metric - and that (i)
applies to the weight of food too. If you tend to think
in pounds and ounces, it's worth brushing up on what the
metric equivalent is before you go shopping for fruit and veg
in markets and supermarkets. Five hundred grams, or half a
kilo, is a common quantity to order, and that converts to just
over a pound (17.65 ounces, to be precise).

YOU MAY SEE...

CONSUMIR PREFERENTEMENTE ANTES DE...	best if used by...
CALORÍAS	calories
SIN GRASA	fat free
CONSERVAR EN FRIGORÍFICO	keep refrigerated
PUEDE CONTENER TRAZAS DE...	may contain traces of...
FECHA LÍMITE DE VENTA...	sell by...
APTO PARA VEGETARIANOS	suitable for vegetarians

measuring cup/spoon	**la taza/la cuchara medidora** *lah tah • thah/lah koo • chah • rah meh • dee • doh • rah*
napkin	**la servilleta** *lah sehr • bee • yeh • tah*
plate	**el plato** *ehl plah • toh*
pot	**la olla** *lah oh • yah*
saucepan	**el cazo** *ehl kah • thoh*
spatula	**la espátula** *lah ehs • pah • too • lah*
spoon	**la cuchara** *lah koo • chah • rah*

For Domestic Items, see page 77.

DRINKS

ESSENTIAL

Can I see the wine list/ drink menu, please?	**La carta de vinos/bebidas, por favor.** *lah <u>kahr</u> • tah deh <u>bee</u> • nohs/ beh • <u>bee</u> • dahs pohr fah • <u>bohr</u>*
What do you recommend?	**¿Qué me recomienda?** *keh meh reh • koh • <u>meeyehn</u> • dah*
I'd like a bottle/glass of red/white wine.	**Quiero una botella/un vaso de vino tinto/blanco.** *<u>keeyeh</u> • roh <u>oo</u> • nah boh • <u>teh</u> • yah/ oon <u>bah</u> • soh deh <u>bee</u> • noh <u>teen</u> • toh/ <u>blahn</u> • koh*
The house wine, please.	**El vino de la casa, por favor.** *ehl <u>bee</u> • noh deh lah <u>kah</u> • sah pohr fah • <u>bohr</u>*
Another bottle/glass, please.	**Otra botella/Otro vaso, por favor.** *<u>oh</u> • trah boh • <u>teh</u> • yah/<u>oh</u> • troh <u>bah</u> • soh pohr fah • <u>bohr</u>*
I'd like a local beer.	**Quiero una cerveza española.** *<u>keeyeh</u> • roh <u>oo</u> • nah thehr • <u>beh</u> • thah*

	ehs • pah • nyoh • lah
Can I buy you a drink?	**¿Puedo invitarle *m*/invitarla *f* a una copa?**
	pweh • doh een • bee • tahr • leh/ een • bee • tahr • lah ah oo • nah koh • pah
Cheers!	**¡Salud!**
	sah • looth
A coffee/tea, please.	**Un café/té, por favor.**
	oon kah • feh/teh pohr fah • bohr
Black.	**Solo.**
	soh • loh
With...	**Con... *kohn...***
milk	**leche**
	leh • cheh
sugar	**azúcar**
	ah • thoo • kahr
artificial sweetener	**edulcorante artificial**
	eh • dool • khoh • rahn • teh ahr • tee • fee • theeyahl
A..., please.	**Un..., por favor.**
	oon...pohr fah • bohr
juice	**zumo**
	thoo • moh
soda	**refresco**
	reh • frehs • koh
water	**agua**
	ah • gwah
sparkling/still	**con/sin gas**
	kohn/seen gahs
Is the tap water safe to drink?	**¿Se puede beber el agua del grifo?**
	seh pweh • deh beh • behr ehl ah • gwah dehl gree • foh

YOU MAY HEAR...

¿Qué desea beber?
keh deh • seh • ah beh • behr

Can I get you
a drink?

¿Con leche o azúcar?
kohn leh • cheh oh ah • thoo • kahr

With milk
or sugar?

¿Agua con gas o sin gas?
ah • gwah kohn gahs oh seen gahs

Sparkling or still
water?

NON-ALCOHOLIC DRINKS

el agua (con/sin gas)
water
ehl ah • gwah (kohn/seen gahs)

(sparkling/still)

el café
ehl kah • feh

coffee

el chocolate caliente
ehl choh • koh • lah • teh kah • leeyehn • teh

hot chocolate

el granizado
ehl grah • nee • thah • doh

iced drink

la horchata
lah ohr • chah • tah

sweet drink made
from tiger
nuts and sugar

la leche
lah leh • cheh

milk

la limonada
lah lee • moh • nah • dah

lemonade

el refresco
ehl reh • frehs • koh

soda

el té (con hielo)
ehl teh (kohn eeyeh • loh)

(iced) tea

el zumo
ehl thoo • moh

juice

APERITIFS, COCKTAILS & LIQUEURS

el coñac
ehl koh•nyahk
brandy

la ginebra
lah khee•neh•brah
gin

el jerez fino
ehl kheh•rehth fee•noh
pale, dry sherry

el jerez oloroso
ehl kheh•rehth oh•loh•roh•soh
dark, heavy sherry

el licor
ehl lee•kohr
liqueur

el oporto
ehl oh•pohr•toh
port

el ron
ehl rohn
rum

la sangría
lah sahn•gree•ah
wine punch

el tequila
ehl teh•kee•lah
tequila

el vodka
ehl bohd•kah
vodka

el whisky
ehl wees•kee
whisky

el whisky escocés
ehl wees•kee ehs•koh•thehs
scotch

Many Spaniards love coffee and drink it throughout the day. Bottled water is available, though tap water is used in the home and is generally safe to drink. Restaurants will almost always serve bottled water with meals, unless you specifically request **agua del grifo** (tap water). Juice is usually served with breakfast.

(i)

There are many popular brands of beer in Spain, including **San Miguel®, Cruzcampo®, Alhambra®, Mahou®, Estrella Damm®** and **Zaragozana®**. Each brand usually has several classes and types of beer available, though most will be a lager-type beer. The classes of beer include **clásica**, a light, pale, pilsner-type lager; **especial**, a heavier pilsner-type lager; **negra**, a dark, malty lager; and **extra**, a heavy, high-alcohol lager.

BEER

la cerveza...	...beer
lah thehr • beh • thah...	
en botella/de barril	bottled/draft
ehn boh • teh • yah/deh bah • rreel	
española/extranjera	local/imported
ehs • pah • nyoh • lah/ehx • trahn • kheh • rah	
negra/ligera	dark/light
neh • grah/lee • kheh • rah	
rubia/pilsner	lager/pilsner
roo • beeyah/peels • nehr	
sin alcohol	non-alcoholic
seen ahl • koh • ohl	

WINE

el cava	sparkling wine
ehl kah • bah	
el champán	champagne
ehl chahm • pahn	
el vino...	...wine
ehl bee • noh...	
de la casa/de mesa	house/table
deh lah kah • sah/deh meh • sah	

With 40 recognized wine regions, Spain has the largest land area under vine in the world and is the third largest producer and exporter of wine. The most well-known types of wine include red wine from Rioja and Ribera del Duero, sherries from Jerez, white wine from Rueda and red wine and white wine from Penedés. Another popular wine, especially in the summer time, is the sparkling white known as **cava**. Spanish wineries are known as **bodegas**; the winemaker is known as a **bodeguero**.

espumoso	sparkling
ehs • poo • moh • soh	
tinto/blanco	red/white
teen • toh/blahn • koh	
seco/dulce	dry/sweet
seh • koh/dool • theh	

For How to Order, see page 192.

ON THE MENU

el aceite *ehl ah • theyee • teh*	oil
el aceite de oliva *ehl ah • theyee • teh deh oh • lee • bah*	olive oil
la aceituna *lah ah • theyee • too • nah*	olive
la acelga *lah ah • thehl • gah*	chard
la achicoria *lah ah • chee • koh • reeyah*	chicory
el agua *ehl ah • gwah*	water
el aguacate *ehl ah • gwah • kah • teh*	avocado
el ajo *ehl ah • khoh*	garlic
el ajo chalote *ehl ah • khoh chah • loh • teh*	shallot
la albahaca *lah ahl • bah • ah • kah*	basil
el albaricoque *ehl ahl • bah • ree • koh • keh*	apricot
la albóndiga *lah ahl • bohn • dee • gah*	meatball
la alcachofa *lah ahl • kah • choh • fah*	artichoke
la alcaparra *lah ahl • kah • pah • rrah*	caper
la alcaravea *lah ahl • kah • rah • beh • ah*	caraway
la almeja *lah ahl • meh • khah*	clam

la almendra
lah ahl • mehn • drah

almond

el almíbar
ehl ahl • mee • bahr

syrup

el anacardo
ehl ah • nah • kahr • doh

cashew

las ancas de rana
lahs ahn • kahs deh rah • nah

frog's legs

la anchoa
lah ahn • choh • ah

anchovy

la anguila
lah ahn • gee • lah

eel

la angula
lah ahn • goo • lah

baby eel

el anís
ehl ah • nees

aniseed

el aperitivo
ehl ah • peh • ree • tee • boh

aperitif

el apio
ehl ah • peeyoh

celery

el arándano
ehl ah • rahn • dah • noh

blueberry

el arándano rojo
ehl ah • rahn • dah • noh roh • khoh

cranberry

el arenque
ehl ah • rehn • keh

herring

el arroz
ehl ah • rrohth

rice

el arroz integral
ehl ah • rrohth een • teh • grahl

whole grain rice

el arroz salvaje
ehl ah • rrohth sahl • bah • kheh

wild rice

el asado
ehl ah • sah • doh

roast

las asaduras
lahs ah • sah • doo • rahs

organ meat [offal]

el atún
ehl ah • toon

tuna

la avellana
lah ah • beh • yah • nah

hazelnut

la avena
lah ah • beh • nah

oat

las aves
lahs ah • behs

poultry

el azafrán
ehl ah • thah • frahn

saffron

el azúcar
ehl ah • thoo • kahr

sugar

el bacalao
bah • kah • lao

cod

los barquillos
lohs bahr • kee • yohs

wafers/ice cream cones

la batata
lah bah • tah • tah

sweet potato

el batido
ehl bah • tee • doh

milk shake

la bebida
lah beh • bee • dah

drink

la berenjena
lah beh • rehn • kheh • nah

eggplant [aubergine]

la berraza
lah beh • rrah • thah

parsnip

el berro
ehl beh • rroh

watercress

la berza
lah behr • thah

kale

el besugo
ehl beh • soo • goh

sea bream

blando
blahn • doh

soft

el bollo
ehl boh • yoh

pastry

el brandy
ehl brahn • dee

brandy

el brécol
ehl breh • kohl

broccoli

los brotes de soja
lohs broh • tehs deh soh • khah

bean sprouts

el buey
ehl bwehy

ox

el buñuelo
ehl boo • nyweh • loh

fritter

la caballa
lah kah • bah • yah

mackerel

la cabra
lah kah • brah

goat

el cabrito
ehl kah • bree • toh

young goat

el cacahuete
ehl kah • kah • weh • teh

peanut

el café
ehl kah • feh

coffee

el café solo — espresso
ehl kah • feh soh • loh

el calabacín — zucchini [courgette]
ehl kah • lah • bah • theen

la calabaza — pumpkin
lah kah • lah • bah • thah

el calamar — squid
ehl kah • lah • mahr

el caldo — broth
ehl kahl • doh

los callos — tripe
lohs kah • yohs

la canela — cinnamon
lah kah • neh • lah

el cangrejo — crab
ehl kahn • greh • khoh

el capuchino — cappuccino
ehl kah • poo • chee • noh

el caracol — snail
ehl kah • rah • kohl

el caramelo — candy [sweet]
ehl kah • rah • meh • loh

la carne — meat
lah kahr • neh

la carne de cangrejo *lah kahr • neh deh* — crabmeat
kahn • greh • khoh

la carne de cerdo *lah kahr • neh deh* — pork
thehr • doh

la carne picada — ground beef
lah kahr • neh pee • kah • dah

la carne de vaca — beef
lah kahr • neh deh bah • kah

el carnero — mutton
ehl kahr • neh • roh

las carrilladas *lahs kah • rree • yah • dahs*	cow's cheeks
casero *kah • seh • roh*	homemade
la castaña *lah kahs • tah • nyah*	chestnut
el cava *ehl kah • bah*	sparkling wine
la caza *lah kah • thah*	game
la cebolla *lah theh • boh • yah*	onion
la cebolleta *lah theh • boh • yeh • tah*	scallion [spring onion]
los cebollinos *lohs theh • boh • yee • nohs*	chives
la cecina de bovino *lah theh • thee • nah deh boh • bee • noh*	corned beef
el centeno *ehl thehn • teh • noh*	rye
el centollo *ehl thehn • toh • yoh*	spider crab
el cereal *ehl theh • reh • ahl*	cereal
la cereza *lah theh • reh • thah*	cherry
la cerveza *lah thehr • beh • thah*	beer
el champiñón *ehl chahm • pee • nyohn*	mushroom
el champán *ehl chahm • pahn*	champagne
la chirivía *lah chee • ree • bee • ah*	parsnip
el chipirón *ehl chee • pee • rohn*	small whole squid

el chocolate — chocolate
ehl choh • koh • lah • teh

el chocolate caliente — hot chocolate
ehl choh • koh • lah • teh kah • leeyehn • teh

el chorizo — highly-seasoned pork sausage
ehl choh • ree • thoh

la chuleta — chop
lah choo • leh • tah

el chuletón — T-bone steak
ehl choo • leh • tohn

el ciervo — deer
ehl theeyehr • boh

la cigala — crayfish
lah thee • gah • lah

el cilantro — cilantro [coriander]
ehl thee • lahn • troh

la ciruela — plum
lah thee • rweh • lah

la ciruela pasa — prune
lah thee • rweh • lah pah • sah

el clavo — clove
ehl klah • boh

el cochinillo — suckling pig
ehl koh • chee • nee • yoh

el coco — coconut
ehl koh • koh

la codorniz — quail
lah koh • dohr • neeth

la col *lah kohl* — cabbage

las coles de Bruselas — Brussels sprouts
lahs koh • lehs deh broo • seh • lahs

la coliflor — cauliflower
lah koh • lee • flohr

el comino — cumin
ehl koh • mee • noh

la compota
lah kohm • poh • tah

stewed fruit

con alcohol
kohn ahl • koh • ohl

with alcohol

con nata
kohn nah • tah

with cream

el condimento
ehl kohn • dee • mehn • toh

relish

el conejo
ehl koh • neh • khoh

rabbit

el congrio
ehl kohn • greeyoh

conger eel

el consomé
ehl kohn • soh • meh

consommé

el coñac
ehl koh • nyahk

brandy

el corazón
ehl koh • rah • thohn

heart

el cordero
ehl kohr • deh • roh

lamb

la cordorniz
lah kohr • dohr • neeth

quail

el coriandro
ehl koh • reeyahn • droh

coriander

la croqueta
lah kroh • keh • tah

croquette

el cruasán
ehl krwah • sahn

croissant

crudo
kroo • doh

raw

los dátiles
lohs dah • tee • lehs

dates

descafeinado
dehs • kah • feyey • nah • doh

decaffeinated

el edulcorante artificial
ehl eh • dool • koh • rahn • teh ahr • tee • fee • theeyahl

artificial sweetener

la empanada
lah ehm • pah • nah • dah

pastry filled with meat, chicken, tuna or vegetables

el encurtido
ehl ehn • koor • tee • doh

pickled

la endibia
lah ehn • dee • beeyah

endive

el eneldo
ehl eh • nehl • doh

dill

la ensalada
lah ehn • sah • lah • dah

salad

la escarola
lah ehs • kah • roh • lah

escarole [chicory]

el espagueti
ehl ehs • pah • geh • tee

spaghetti

la espaldilla
lah ehs • pahl • dee • yah

shoulder

el espárrago
ehl ehs • pah • rrah • goh

asparagus

las especias
lahs ehs • peh • theeyahs

spices

la espinaca
lah ehs • pee • nah • kah

spinach

el estragón
ehl ehs • trah • gohn

tarragon

el faisán
ehl fayee • sahn

pheasant

la falda de ternera
lah fahl • dah deh tehr • neh • rah

beef brisket

los fiambres
lohs feeyahm • brehs

cold cuts [charcuterie]

el fideo
ehl fee • deh • oh

noodle

el filete
ehl fee • leh • teh

steak

el flan
ehl flahn

caramel custard

el fletán
ehl fleh • tahn

halibut

la frambuesa
lah frahm • bweh • sah

raspberry

la fresa
lah freh • sah

strawberry

la fruta
lah froo • tah

fruit

los frutos secos
lohs froo • tohs seh • kohs

nuts

la galleta
lah gah • yeh • tah

cookie [biscuit]

la galleta salada
lah gah • yeh • tah sah • lah • dah

cracker

la gamba
lah gahm • bah

shrimp

el ganso
ehl gahn • soh

wild goose

el garbanzo
ehl gahr • bahn • thoh

chickpea

el gazpacho
ehl gahth • pah • choh

cold tomato-based soup

la ginebra
lah khee • neh • brah

gin

el gofre
ehl goh • freh

waffle

la granada
lah grah • nah • dah

pomegranate

el granizado
ehl grah • nee • thah • doh

iced drink

la grosella espinosa
lah groh • seh • yah ehs • pee • noh • sah

gooseberry

la grosella negra
lah groh • seh • yah neh • grah

black currant

la grosella roja
lah groh • seh • yah roh • khah

red currant

la guayaba
lah gwah • yah • bah

guava

la guinda
lah geen • dah

sour cherry

la guindilla en polvo
lah geen • dee • yah ehn pohl • boh

chili pepper

el guirlache
ehl geer • lah • cheh

nougat

el guisante
ehl gee • sahn • teh

pea

la hamburguesa
lah ahm • boor • geh • sah

hamburger

la harina
lah ah • ree • nah

flour

la harina de avena
lah ah • ree • nah deh ah • beh • nah

oatmeal

la harina de maíz	cornmeal
lah ah • <u>ree</u> • nah deh mah • <u>eeth</u>	
el helado	ice cream
ehl eh • <u>lah</u> • doh	
el (cubito de) hielo	ice (cube)
ehl (kooh • <u>bee</u> • toh deh) <u>eeyeh</u> • loh	
el hígado	liver
ehl <u>ee</u> • gah • doh	
el higo	fig
ehl <u>ee</u> • goh	
el hinojo	fennel
ehl ee • <u>noh</u> • khoh	
la hoja de laurel	bay leaf
lah <u>oh</u> • khah deh lawoo • <u>rehl</u>	
el hueso	bone
ehl <u>weh</u> • soh	
el huevo	egg
ehl <u>weh</u> • boh	
el jabalí	wild boar
ehl khah • bah • <u>lee</u>	
la jalea	jelly
lah khah • <u>leh</u> • ah	
el jamón	ham
ehl khah • <u>mohn</u>	

el jengibre
ehl khehn • khee • breh
ginger

el jerez
ehl kheh • rehth
sherry

la judía
lah khoo • dee • ah
bean

la judía verde
lah khoo • dee • ah behr • deh
green bean

el ketchup
ehl keht • choop
ketchup

el kiwi
ehl kee • wee
kiwi

el lacón
ehl lah • kohn
pork shoulder

la langosta
lah lahn • gohs • tah
lobster

el lavanco
ehl lah • bahn • koh
wild duck

la leche
lah leh • cheh
milk

la leche de soja
lah leh • cheh deh soh • khah
soymilk
[soya milk]

la lechuga
lah leh • choo • gah
lettuce

la lengua
lah lehn • gwah
tongue

el lenguado
ehl lehn • gwah • doh
sole

la lenteja
lah lehn • teh • khah
lentil

el licor
ehl lee • kohr
liqueur

el licor de naranja
ehl lee • kohr deh nah • rahn • khah
orange liqueur

los licores *lohs lee • kohr • ehs*	spirits
la liebre *lah leyee • breh*	hare
la lima *lah lee • mah*	lime
el limón *ehl lee • mohn*	lemon
la limonada *lah leeh • moh • nah • dah*	lemonade
la lombarda *lah lohm • bahr • dah*	red cabbage
el lomo *ehl loh • moh*	loin
la lubina *lah loo • bee • nah*	(sea) bass
los macarrones *lohs mah • kah • rrohn • ehs*	macaroni
la magdalena *lah mahg • dah • leh • nah*	muffin
la maicena *lah mayee • theh • nah*	cornmeal
el maíz *ehl mah • eeth*	sweet corn
la mandarina *lah mahn • dah • ree • nah*	tangerine
el mango *ehl mahn • goh*	mango
las manos de cerdo *lahs mah • nohs deh thehr • doh*	pig's feet [trotters]
la mantequilla *lah mahn • teh • kee • yah*	butter
la manzana *lah mahn • thah • nah*	apple

la margarina
lah mahr • gah • ree • nah   margarine

el marisco
ehl mah • rees • koh   shellfish

la mayonesa
lah mah • yoh • neh • sah   mayonnaise

el mazapán
ehl mah • thah • pahn   marzipan

el mejillón
ehl meh • khee • yohn   mussel

la mejorana
lah meh • khoh • rah • nah   marjoram

la melaza
lah meh • lah • thah   molasses

el melocotón
ehl meh • loh • koh • tohn   peach

el melón
ehl meh • lohn   melon

la menta
lah mehn • tah   mint

el menudillo
ehl meh • noo • dee • yoh   giblet

el merengue
ehl meh • rehn • geh   meringue

la merluza
lah mehr • loo • thah   hake

la mermelada
lah mehr • meh • lah • dah   marmalade/jam

el mero
ehl meh • roh   grouper

la miel
lah meeyehl   honey

la molleja
lah moh • yeh • khah   sweetbread

la morcilla
lah mohr • thee • yah
black pudding

la mostaza
lah mohs • tah • thah
mustard

el muesli
ehl mwehs • lee
granola [muesli]

el nabo
ehl nah • boh
turnip

la naranja
lah nah • rahn • khah
orange

la nata
lah nah • tah
cream

la nata agria
lah nah • tah ah • greeyah
sour cream

la nata montada
lah nah • tah mohn • tah • dah
whipped cream

las natillas
lahs nah • tee • yahs
custard

la nuez
lah nwehth
walnut

la nuez moscada
lah nwehth mohs • kah • dah
nutmeg

el oporto
ehl oh • pohr • toh
port

el orégano
ehl oh • reh • gah • noh
oregano

la ostra
lah ohs • trah
oyster

la pacana
lah pah • kah • nah
pecan

la paella
lah pah • eh • yah
rice dish

la paletilla
lah pah • leh • tee • yah
shank

el palmito — palm heart
ehl pahl•mee•toh

el pan — bread
ehl pahn

el panecillo — roll
ehl pah•neh•thee•yoh

la papaya — papaya
lah pah•pah•yah

la paprika — paprika
lah pah•pree•kah

la pasa — raisin
lah pah•sah

la pasta — pasta
lah pahs•tah

el pastel — pie
ehl pahs•tehl

el pastel de queso — cheesecake
ehl pahs•tehl deh keh•soh

la pata — leg
lah pah•tah

la patata — potato
lah pah•tah•tah

las patatas fritas — French fries
lahs pah•tah•tahs free•tahs

las patatas fritas — potato chips [crisps]
lahs pah•tah•tahs free•tahs

el paté — pâté
ehl pah•teh

el pato — duck
ehl pah•toh

el pavo — turkey
ehl pah•boh

la pechuga (de pollo) — breast (of chicken)
lah peh•choo•gah (deh poh•yoh)

el pepinillo — pickle

ehl peh • pee • nee • yoh
el pepino — cucumber

ehl peh • pee • noh
la pera — pear

lah peh • rah
la perca — sea perch

lah pehr • kah
la perdiz — partridge

lah pehr • deeth
el perejil — parsley

ehl peh • reh • kheel
el perrito caliente — hot dog

ehl peh • rree • toh kah • leeyehn • teh
el pescadito — small fish

ehl pehs • kah • dee • toh
el pescado — fish

ehl pehs • kah • doh
el pescado frito — fried fish

ehl pehs • kah • doh free • toh
pescado y marisco — seafood

pehs • kah • doh ee mah • rees • koh
el pez espada — swordfish

ehl peth ehs • pah • dah
el pichón — young pigeon

ehl pee • chohn
pilsner — pilsner (beer)

peels • nehr
el pimentón — paprika

ehl pee • mehn • tohn
la pimienta — pepper (seasoning)

lah pee • meeyehn • tah
la pimienta negra — black pepper

lah pee • meeyehn • tah neh • grah
la pimienta inglesa — allspice

lah pee • meeyehn • tah een • gleh • sah

el pimiento   pepper (vegetable)
ehl pee • meeyehn • toh

la piña   pineapple
lah pee • nyah

los piñones   pine nuts
lohs pee • nyohn • ehs

la pintada   guinea fowl
lah peen • tah • dah

la pizza   pizza
lah peeth • thah

el plátano   banana
ehl plah • tah • noh

el pollo   chicken
ehl poh • yoh

el pollo frito   fried chicken
ehl poh • yoh free • toh

el pomelo   grapefruit
ehl poh • meh • loh

el puerro   leek
ehl pweh • rroh

el pulpo   octopus
ehl pool • poh

el queso   cheese
ehl keh • soh

el queso de cabra   goat cheese
ehl keh • soh deh kah • brah

el queso crema   cream cheese
ehl keh • soh kreh • mah

el queso roquefort   blue cheese
ehl keh • soh roh • keh • fohrt

el rábano   radish
ehl rah • bah • noh

el rabo de buey   oxtail
ehl rah • boh deh bwehy

el rape   monkfish

ehl <u>rah</u> • peh

el ravioli — ravioli
ehl rah • <u>beeyoh</u> • lee

la raya — skate
lah <u>rah</u> • yah

el refresco — soda
ehl reh • <u>frehs</u> • koh

relleno — stuffed/stuffing
reh • <u>yeh</u> • noh

la remolacha — beet
lah reh • moh • <u>lah</u> • chah

el repollo — cabbage
ehl reh • <u>poh</u> • yoh

el requesón — cottage cheese
ehl reh • keh • <u>sohn</u>

el requesón de soja — tofu
ehl reh • keh • <u>sohn</u> deh <u>soh</u> • khah

los retoños de bambú — bamboo shoots
lohs reh • <u>toh</u> • nyohs deh bahm • <u>boo</u>

el riñón — kidney
ehl ree • <u>nyohn</u>

el róbalo — haddock
ehl <u>roh</u> • bah • loh

el romero — rosemary
ehl roh • <u>meh</u> • roh

el ron — rum
ehl rohn

el rosbif — roast beef
ehl rohs • <u>beef</u>

la rosquilla — doughnut
lah rohs • <u>kee</u> • yah

rubia — lager (beer)
<u>roo</u> • beeyah

el ruibarbo — rhubarb
ehl rwee • <u>bahr</u> • boh

la sal
lah sahl

salt

el salami
ehl sah • lah • mee

salami

la salchicha
lah sahl • chee • chah

sausage

el salmón
ehl sahl • mohn

salmon

el salmonete
ehl sahl • moh • neh • teh

red mullet

la salsa
lah sahl • sah

sauce

la salsa agridulce
lah sahl • sah ah • gree • dool • theh

sweet and sour sauce

la salsa alioli
lah sahl • sah ah • yee • oh • lee

garlic sauce

la salsa picante
lah sahl • sah pee • kahn • teh

hot pepper sauce

la salsa de soja
lah sahl • sah deh soh • khah

soy sauce

la salvia
lah sahl • beeyah

sage

la sandía
lah sahn • dee • ah

watermelon

el sándwich
ehl sahnd • weech

sandwich

la sangría
lah sahn • gree • ah

wine punch

la sardina
lah sahr • dee • nah

sardine

la semilla
lah seh • mee • yah

seed

la semilla de soja
lah seh • mee • yah deh soh • khah

soybean [soya bean]

el sésamo

sesame

ehl seh • sah • moh

los sesos — brains

lohs seh • sohs

la seta — mushroom

lah seh • tah

la sidra — cider

lah see • drah

el sifón — seltzer water

ehl see • fohn

el sirope — syrup

ehl see • roh • peh

la soja — soy [soya]

lah soh • khah

el solomillo — sirloin

ehl soh • loh • mee • yoh

la sopa — soup

lah soh • pah

el sorbete — sorbet

ehl sohr • beh • teh

el suero de leche — buttermilk

ehl sweh • roh deh leh • cheh

la tarta — cake

lah tahr • tah

el té — tea

ehl teh

la ternera — veal

lah tehr • neh • rah

el tequila — tequila

ehl teh • kee • lah

el tiburón — shark

ehl tee • boo • rohn

tinto — red (wine)

teen • toh

el tocino — bacon

ehl toh • thee • noh

el tofu — tofu
ehl toh • foo

el tomate — tomato
ehl toh • mah • teh

el tomillo — thyme
ehl toh • mee • yoh

la tónica — tonic water
lah toh • nee • kah

la tortilla — omelet
lah tohr • tee • yah

la tortita — large pancake served as an afternoon snack
lah tohr • tee • tah

la tostada — toast
lah tohs • tah • dah

el trigo — wheat
ehl tree • goh

la trucha — trout
lah troo • chah

las trufas — truffles
lahs troo • fahs

la uva — grape
lah oo • bah

la vainilla — vanilla
lah bayee • nee • yah

el venado — venison
ehl beh • nah • doh

la verdura — vegetable
lah behr • doo • rah

el vermut — vermouth
ehl behr • moot

las vieiras — scallop
lahs bee • eyee • rahs

el vinagre — vinegar
ehl bee • nah • greh

el vino	wine
ehl beeh • noh	
el vino dulce	dessert wine
ehl bee • noh dool • theh	
el vodka	vodka
ehl bohd • kah	
el whisky	whisky
ehl wees • kee	
el whisky escocés	scotch
ehl wees • kee ehs • koh • thehs	
la yema/clara de huevo	egg yolk/white
lah yeh • mah/klah • rah deh weh • boh	
el yogur	yogurt
ehl yoh • goor	
la zanahoria	carrot
lah thah • nah • oh • reeyah	
la zarzamora	blackberry
lah thahr • thah • moh • rah	
el zumo	juice
ehl thoo • moh	

GOING OUT

GOING OUT

ESSENTIAL

What's there to do at night?	**¿Qué se puede hacer por las noches?** *keh seh <u>pweh</u>•deh ah•<u>thehr</u> pohr lahs <u>noh</u>•chehs*
Do you have a program of events?	**¿Tiene un programa de espectáculos?** *<u>teeyeh</u>•neh oon proh•<u>grah</u>•mah deh ehs•pehk•<u>tah</u>•koo•lohs*
What's playing tonight?	**¿Qué hay en cartelera esta noche?** *keh aye ehn kahr•teh•<u>leh</u>•rah ehs•tah <u>noh</u>•cheh*
Where's…?	**¿Dónde está…?** *<u>dohn</u>•deh ehs•<u>tah</u>…*
the downtown area	**el centro** *ehl <u>thehn</u>•troh*
the bar	**el bar** *ehl bahr*
the dance club	**la discoteca** *lah dees•koh•<u>teh</u>•kah*

Is there a cover charge?	**¿Hay que pagar entrada?** *aye keh pah • gahr ehn • trah • dah*

> (i)
>
> Spain is famous for its centuries-old tradition of bullfighting. Known as **tauromaquia** or **corrida de toros**, bullfighting is seen as an art and tradition by many, and as a cruel and violent act against animals by others. Whether you find it fascinating or appalling, the bullfight is a unique experience in Spain. The bullfighting season runs from March to October; many towns have a vibrant festival in March to open the season.

ENTERTAINMENT

Can you recommend…?	**¿Puede recomendarme…?** *pweh • deh reh • koh • mehn • dahr • meh…*
a concert	**un concierto** *oon kohn • theeyehr • toh*
a movie	**una película** *oo • nah peh • lee • koo • lah*
an opera	**una ópera** *oo • nah oh • peh • rah*
a play	**una obra de teatro** *oo • nah oh • brah deh teh • ah • troh*
When does it start/end?	**¿A qué hora empieza/termina?** *ah keh oh • rah ehm • peeyeh • thah/ tehr • mee • nah*
What's the dress code?	**¿Cómo hay que ir vestido m/vestida f?** *koh • moh aye keh eer behs • tee • doh/ behs • tee • dah*
I like…	**Me gusta…** *meh goos • tah…*

YOU MAY HEAR...

Por favor apaguen sus teléfonos móviles. Turn off your cell
pohr fah • bohr ah • pah • gehn soos [mobile] phones,
teh • leh • foh • nohs moh • bee • lehs please.

classical music	**la música clásica**
	lah moo • see • kah klah • see • kah
folk music	**la música folk**
	lah moo • see • kah folk
jazz	**el jazz**
	ehl jazz
pop music	**la música pop**
	lah moo • see • kah pop
rap	**el rap**
	ehl rap

For Tickets, see page 43.

NIGHTLIFE

What's there to do at night?	**¿Qué se puede hacer por las noches?**
	keh seh pweh • deh ah • thehr pohr lahs noh • chehs
Can you recommend...?	**¿Puede recomendarme...?**
	pweh • deh reh • koh • mehn • dahr • meh...
a bar	**un bar**
	oon bahr
a cabaret	**un cabaré**
	oon kah • bah • reh
a casino	**un casino**
	oon kah • see • noh
a dance club	**una discoteca**
	oo • nah dees • koh • teh • kah

ⓘ

One of Spain's greatest cultural achievements is the **flamenco**. A combination of music, song and dance, the **flamenco** is an emotional performance that should not be missed when you are in Spain. Major cities such as Madrid, Seville and other Andalucian towns have **flamenco** performances year round. A **peña** is a small, intimate membership club (some allow guests) where you can view **flamenco** performed. **Tablaos** are typical public venues for **flamenco**. Seeing **flamenco** at a **tablao** can be an expensive night out, but well worth the money.

a flamenco performance	**un espectáculo de flamenco** *oon ehs • pehk • tah • koo • loh deh flah • mehn • koh*
a gay club	**una discoteca gay** *oo • nah dees • koh • teh • kah gay*
a jazz club	**un club de jazz** *oon kloob deh jazz*
a club with Spanish music	**un bar con música española** *oon bahr kohn moo • see • kah ehs • pah • nyoh • lah*
Is there live music?	**¿Hay música en vivo?** *aye moo • see • kah ehn bee • boh*
How do I get there?	**¿Cómo se llega allí?** *koh • moh seh yeh • gah ah • yee*
Is there a cover charge?	**¿Hay que pagar entrada?** *aye keh pah • gahr ehn • trah • dah*
Let's go dancing.	**Vamos a bailar.** *bah • mohs ah bayee • lahr*
Is this area safe at night?	**¿Esta zona es segura por la noche?** *ehs • tah tho • nah ehs seh • goo • rah pohr lah noh • cheh*

ROMANCE

ESSENTIAL

Would you like to go out for a drink/dinner?	**¿Le gustaría salir a tomar una copa/cenar?**
	leh goos • tah • ree • ah sah • leer ah toh • mahr oo • nah koh • pah/ theh • nahr
What are your plans for tonight/tomorrow?	**¿Qué planes tiene para esta noche/mañana?**
	keh plah • nehs teeyeh • nehs pah • rah ehs • tah noh • cheh/mah • nyah • nah
Can I have your number?	**¿Puede darme su número?**
	pweh • deh dahr • meh soo noo • meh • roh
Can I join you?	**¿Puedo acompañarle** m/**acompañarla** f**?**
	pweh • doh ah • kohm • pah • nyahr • leh/ ah • kohm • pah • nyahr • lah
Can I buy you a drink?	**¿Puedo invitarle** m/**invitarla** f **a una copa?**

	pweh • doh een • bee • tahr • leh/
	een • bee • tahr • lah ah oo • nah
	koh • pah
I like you.	**Me gustas.**
	meh goos • tahs
I love you.	**Te quiero.**
	teh keeyeh • roh

THE DATING GAME

Would you like to go out for...?	**¿Le gustaría ir...?**
	leh goos • tah • ree • ah eer...
coffee	**a tomar un café**
	ah toh • mahr oon kah • feh
a drink	**a tomar un copa**
	ah toh • mahr oo • nah koh • pah
dinner	**a cenar**
	ah theh • nahr
What are your plans for...?	**¿Qué planes tiene para...?**
	keh plahn • ehs teeyeh • neh pah • rah...
today	**hoy**
	oy
tonight	**esta noche**
	ehs • tah noh • cheh
tomorrow	**mañana**
	mah • nyah • nah
this weekend	**este fin de semana**
	ehs • teh feen deh seh • mah • nah
Where would you like to go?	**¿Adónde le gustaría ir?**
	ah dohn • deh leh goos • tah • ree • ah eer
I'd like to go to...	**Me gustaría ir a...**
	meh goos • tah • ree • ah eer ah...
Do you like...?	**¿Le gusta...?**
	leh goos • tah...

Can I have your number/e-mail?	**¿Puede darme su número/dirección de correo electrónico?**
	pweh • deh dahr • meh soo noo • meh • roh/ dee • eh • rehk • theeyohn deh koh • rreh • oh eh • lehk • troh • nee • koh
Are you on Facebook/Twitter?	**¿Está en Facebook/Twitter?** _(polite form)_
	ehs • tah ehn Facebook/Twitter
	¿Estás en Facebook/Twitter? _(informal form)_
	ehs • tahs ehn Facebook/Twitter
Can I join you?	**¿Puedo acompañarle** m/**acompañarla** f**?**
	pweh • doh ah • kohm • pah • nyahr • leh/ ah • kohm • pah • nyahr • lah
You're very attractive.	**Eres muy guapo** m/**guapa** f**.**
	eh • rehs mooy gwah • poh/gwah • pah
Let's go somewhere quieter.	**Vayamos a un sitio más tranquilo.**
	bah • yah • mohs ah oon see • teeyoh mahs trahn • kee • loh

For Communications, see page 81.

ACCEPTING & REJECTING

I'd love to.	**Me encantaría.**
	meh ehn • kahn • tah • ree • yah
Where should we meet?	**¿Dónde quedamos?**
	dohn • deh keh • dah • mohs
I'll meet you at the bar/your hotel.	**Quedamos en el bar/su hotel.**
	keh • dah • mohs ehn ehl bahr/soo oh • tehl
I'll come by at…	**Pasaré a recogerle** m/**recogerla** f **a las…**
	pah • sah • reh ah reh • koh • khehr • leh/ reh • koh • khehr • lah ah lahs…
What is your address?	**¿Cuál es su dirección?** _kwahl ehs soo dee • rehk • theeyohn_

I'm busy.	**Estoy ocupado** m/**ocupada** f.
	ehs • <u>toy</u> oh • koo • <u>pah</u> • doh/
	oh • koo • <u>pah</u> • dah
I'm not interested.	**No me interesa.** noh meh
	een • teh • <u>reh</u> • sah
Leave me alone.	**Déjeme en paz.**
	<u>deh</u> • kheh • meh ehn pahth
Stop bothering me!	**¡Deje de molestarme!**
	<u>deh</u> • kheh deh moh • lehs • <u>tahr</u> • meh

For Time, see page 23.

GETTING INTIMATE

Can I hug/kiss you?	**¿Puedo abrazarte/besarte?**
	<u>pweh</u> • doh ah • brah • <u>thahr</u> • teh/
	beh • <u>sahr</u> • teh
Yes.	**Sí.** see
No.	**No.** noh
Stop!	**¡Para!** <u>pah</u> • rah
I love you.	**Te quiero.** teh <u>keeyeh</u> • roh

SEXUAL PREFERENCES

Are you gay?	**¿Eres gay?**
	<u>eh</u> • rehs gay
I'm…	**Soy…** soy…
heterosexual	**heterosexual**
	eh • teh • roh • sehks • <u>wahl</u>
homosexual	**homosexual**
	oh • moh • sehks • <u>wahl</u>
bisexual	**bisexual**
	bee • sehks • <u>wahl</u>
Do you like	**¿Te gustan los hombres/las mujeres?**
men/women?	teh <u>goos</u> • tahn lohs <u>ohm</u> • brehs/
	lahs moo • <u>kheh</u> • rehs

DICTIONARY

ENGLISH–SPANISH

A

abbey la abadía
accept v aceptar
access el acceso
accident el accidente
accommodation el alojamiento
account la cuenta
acupuncture la acupuntura
adapter el adaptador
address la dirección
admission la entrada
after después; **~noon** la tarde; **~shave** el bálsamo para después del afeitado
age la edad
agency la agencia
AIDS el sida
air el aire; **~ conditioning** el aire acondicionado; **~ pump** el aire; **~line** la compañía aérea; **~mail** el correo aéreo; **~plane** el avión; **~port** el aeropuerto
aisle el pasillo; **~ seat** el asiento de pasillo
allergic alérgico; **~ reaction** la reacción alérgica

allow v permitir
alone solo
alter v **(clothing)** hacer un arreglo
alternate route el otro camino
aluminum foil el papel de aluminio
amazing increíble
ambulance la ambulancia
American estadounidense
amusement park el parque de atracciones
anemic anémico
anesthesia la anestesia
animal el animal
ankle el tobillo
antibiotic el antibiótico
antiques store la tienda de -antigüedades
antiseptic cream la crema antiséptica
anything algo
apartment el apartamento
appendix (body part) el apéndice
appetizer el aperitivo
appointment la cita
arcade el salón de

adj adjective	**BE** British English	**v** verb
adv adverb	**n** noun	

juegos recreativos

area code el prefijo

arm el brazo

aromatherapy la aromaterapia

around (the corner) doblando (la esquina)

arrivals (airport) las llegadas

arrive v llegar

artery la arteria

arthritis la artritis

arts las letras

Asian asiático

aspirin la aspirina

asthmatic asmático

ATM el cajero automático

attack el asalto

attend v asistir

attraction (place) el sitio de interés

attractive guapo

Australia Australia

Australian australiano

automatic automático; ~ **car** coche automático

available disponible

B

baby el bebé; ~ **bottle** el biberón; ~ **wipe** la toallita; ~**sitter** el/la canguro

back la espalda; ~**ache** el dolor de espalda; ~**pack** la mochila

bag la maleta

baggage el equipaje; ~ **claim** la recogida de equipajes; ~ **ticket** el talón de equipaje

bakery la panadería

ballet el ballet

bandage la tirita

bank el banco

bar el bar

barbecue la barbacoa

barber la peluquería de caballeros

baseball el béisbol

basket (grocery store) la cesta

basketball el baloncesto

bathroom el baño

battery (car) la batería

battery la pila

battleground el campo de batalla

be v ser, estar

beach la playa

beautiful precioso

bed la cama; ~ **and breakfast** la pensión

begin v empezar

before antes de

beginner principiante

behind detrás de

beige beis

belt el cinturón

berth la litera

best el/la mejor

better mejor

bicycle la bicicleta

big grande
bigger más grande
bike route el sendero para bicicletas
bikini el biquini; **~ wax** la depilación de las ingles
bill v (charge) cobrar; **~ n** (money) el billete; **~ n** (of sale) el recibo
bird el pájaro
birthday el cumpleaños
black negro
bladder la vejiga
bland soso
blanket la manta
bleed v sangrar
blood la sangre; **~ pressure** la tensión arterial
blouse la blusa
blue azul
board v embarcar
boarding pass la tarjeta de embarque
boat el barco
bone el hueso
book el libro; **~store** la librería
boots las botas
boring aburrido
botanical garden el jardín botánico
bother v molestar
bottle la botella; **~ opener** el abrebotellas
bowl el cuenco
box la caja

boxing match la pelea de boxeo
boy el niño; **~friend** el novio
bra el sujetador
bracelet la pulsera
brakes (car) los frenos
break v romper
break-in (burglary) el allanamiento de morada
breakdown la avería
breakfast el desayuno
breast el seno; **~feed** dar el pecho
breathe v respirar
bridge el puente
briefs (clothing) los calzoncillos
bring v traer
British británico
broken roto
brooch el broche
broom la escoba
brother el hermano
brown marrón
bug el insecto
building el edificio
burn v (CD) grabar
bus el autobús; **~ station** la estación de autobuses; **~ stop** la parada de autobús; **~ ticket** el billete de autobús; **~ tour** el recorrido en autobús
business los negocios; **~ card** la tarjeta de negocios;

~ **center** el centro de negocios; ~ **class** la clase preferente; ~ **hours** el horario de atención al público

butcher el carnicero

buttocks las nalgas

buy v comprar

bye adiós

C

cabaret el cabaré

cabin (house) la cabaña; ~ **(ship)** el camarote

cable car el teleférico

cafe la cafetería

call v llamar; ~ n la llamada

calories las calorías

camera la cámara; **digital** ~ la cámara digital; ~ **case** la funda para la cámara; ~ **store** la tienda de fotografía

camp v acampar; ~ **stove** el hornillo; ~**site** el cámping

can opener el abrelatas

Canada Canadá

Canadian canadiense

cancel v cancelar

candy el caramelo

canned goods las conservas

canyon el cañón

car el coche; ~ **hire [BE]** el alquiler de coches; ~ **park [BE]** el aparcamiento; ~ **rental** el alquiler de coches; ~ **seat** el asiento de niño

carafe la garrafa

card la tarjeta; **ATM** ~ la tarjeta de cajero automático; **credit** ~ la tarjeta de crédito; **debit** ~ la tarjeta de débito; **phone** ~ la tarjeta telefónica

carry-on (piece of hand luggage) el equipaje de mano

cart (grocery store) el carrito; ~ **(luggage)** el carrito para el equipaje

carton el cartón; ~ **of cigarettes** el cartón de tabaco

case (amount) la caja

cash v cobrar; ~ n el efectivo; ~ **advance** sacar dinero de la tarjeta

cashier el cajero

casino el casino

castle el castillo

cathedral la catedral

cave la cueva

CD el CD

cell phone el teléfono móvil

Celsius el grado centígrado

centimeter el centímetro

certificate el certificado

chair la silla; ~ **lift** la telesilla

change v **(buses)** cambiar; ~ n **(money)** el cambio

charcoal el carbón

charge v (**credit card**) cobrar;
~ n (**cost**) el precio
cheap barato
cheaper más barato
check v (**on something**)
revisar; ~ v (**luggage**)
facturar; ~ n (**payment**) el
cheque; ~-**in** (**airport**) la
facturación; ~-**in** (**hotel**)
el registro; ~**ing account**
la cuenta corriente; ~-**out**
(**hotel**) la salida
Cheers! ¡Salud!
chemical toilet el váter
químico
chemist [BE] la farmacia
cheque [BE] el cheque
chest (**body part**) el pecho;
~ **pain** el dolor de pecho
chewing gum el chicle
child el niño; ~ **seat** la silla
para niños
children's menu el menú para
niños
children's portion la ración
para niños
Chinese chino
chopsticks los palillos chinos
church la iglesia
cigar el puro
cigarette el cigarrillo
class la clase; **business ~** la
clase preferente; **economy ~**
la clase económica; **first ~** la
primera clase

classical music la música
clásica
clean v limpiar; ~ adj limpio;
~**ing product** el producto de
limpieza; ~**ing supplies** los
productos de limpieza
clear v (**on an ATM**) borrar
cliff el acantilado
cling film [BE] el film
transparente
close v (**a shop**) cerrar
closed cerrado
clothing la ropa; ~ **store** la
tienda de ropa
club la discoteca
coat el abrigo
coffee shop la cafetería
coin la moneda
colander el escurridor
cold n (**sickness**) el catarro;
~ adj (**temperature**) frío
colleague el compañero de
trabajo
cologne la colonia
color el color
comb el peine
come v venir
complaint la queja
computer el ordenador
concert el concierto; ~ **hall** la
sala de conciertos
condition (**medical**) el estado
de salud
conditioner el suavizante
condom el preservativo

conference la conferencia
confirm v confirmar
congestion la congestión
connect v (internet) conectarse
connection (internet) la conexión; ~ (flight) la conexión de vuelo
constipated estreñido
consulate el consulado
consultant el consultor
contact v ponerse en contacto con
contact lens la lentilla de contacto; ~ **solution** el líquido de lentillas de contacto
contagious contagioso
convention hall el salón de congresos
conveyor belt la cinta transportadora
cook v cocinar
cooking gas el gas butano
cool (temperature) frío
copper el cobre
corkscrew el sacacorchos
cost v costar
cot el catre
cotton el algodón
cough v toser; ~ n la tos
country code el código de país
cover charge la entrada
crash v (car) estrellarse
cream (ointment) la pomada

credit card la tarjeta de crédito
crew neck el cuello redondo
crib la cuna
crystal el cristal
cup la taza
currency la moneda; ~ **exchange** el cambio de divisas; ~ **exchange office** la casa de cambio
current account [BE] la cuenta corriente
customs las aduanas
cut v (hair) cortar; ~ n (injury) el corte
cute mono
cycling el ciclismo

D

damage v causar daño
damaged ha sufrido daños
dance v bailar; ~ **club** la discoteca
dangerous peligroso
dark oscuro
date (calendar) la fecha
day el día
deaf sordo
debit card la tarjeta de débito
deck chair la tumbona
declare v declarar
decline v (credit card) rechazar
deeply hondo
degrees (temperature) los

grados

delay v retrasarse

delete v (computer) borrar

delicatessen la charcutería

delicious delicioso

denim tela vaquero

dentist el dentista

denture la dentadura

deodorant el desodorante

department store los grandes almacenes

departures (airport) las salidas

deposit v depositar; ~ n (bank) el depósito bancario; ~ v (reserve a room) la fianza

desert el desierto

dessert el postre

detergent el detergente

develop v (film) revelar

diabetic diabético

dial v marcar

diamond el diamante

diaper el pañal

diarrhea la diarrea

diesel el diesel

difficult difícil

digital digital; ~ **camera** la cámara digital; ~ **photos** las fotos digitales; ~ **prints** las fotos digitales

dining room el comedor

dinner la cena

direction la dirección

dirty sucio

disabled discapacitado; ~ **accessible [BE]** el acceso para discapacitados

discharge (bodily fluid) la secreción

disconnect (computer) desconectar

discount el descuento

dish (kitchen) el plato; ~**washer** el lavavajillas; ~**washing liquid** el líquido lavavajillas

display v mostrar; ~ **case** la vitrina

disposable desechable; ~ **razor** la cuchilla desechable

dive v bucear

diving equipment el equipo de buceo

divorce v divorciar

dizzy mareado

doctor el médico

doll la muñeca

dollar (U.S.) el dólar

domestic nacional; ~ **flight** el vuelo nacional

door la puerta

dormitory el dormitorio

double bed la cama de matrimonio

downtown el centro

dozen la docena

drag lift el telesquí

dress (piece of clothing)
el vestido; ~ **code** las normas
de vestuario

drink v beber; ~ n la bebida;
~ **menu** la carta de bebidas;
~ing **water** el agua potable

drive v conducir

driver's license number
el número de permiso de
conducir

drop (medicine) la gota

drowsiness la somnolencia

dry cleaner la tintorería

dubbed doblada

during durante

duty (tax) el impuesto; ~-**free**
libre de impuestos

DVD el DVD

E

ear la oreja; ~**ache** el dolor
de oído

earlier más temprano

early temprano

earrings los pendientes

east el este

easy fácil

eat v comer

economy class la clase
económica

elbow el codo

electric outlet el enchufe
eléctrico

elevator el ascensor

e-mail v enviar un correo
electrónico; ~ n el correo
electrónico; ~ **address**
la dirección de correo
electrónico

emergency la emergencia;
~ **exit** la salida de urgencia

empty v vaciar

enamel (jewelry) el esmalte

end v terminar

English el inglés

engrave v grabar

enjoy v disfrutar

enter v entrar

entertainment el
entretenimiento

entrance la entrada

envelope el sobre

equipment el equipo

escalators las escaleras
mecánicas

e-ticket el billete electrónico

EU resident el/la residente
de la UE

euro el euro

evening la noche

excess el exceso

exchange v (money) cambiar;
~ v (goods) devolver;
~ n (place) la casa de
cambio; ~ **rate** el tipo de
cambio

excursion la excursión

excuse v (to get past) pedir
perdón; ~ v (to get attention)
disculparse

exhausted agotado
exit v salir; ~ n la salida
expensive caro
expert (skill level) experto
exposure (film) la foto
express rápido; ~ **bus** el
   autobús rápido; ~ **train** el
   tren rápido
extension (phone) la
   extensión
extra adicional; ~ **large** equis
   ele (XL)
extract v **(tooth)** extraer
eye el ojo
eyebrow wax la depilación de
   cejas

F

face la cara
facial la limpieza de cutis
family la familia
fan (appliance) el ventilador;
   ~ **(souvenir)** el abanico
far lejos; **~-sighted**
   hipermétrope
farm la granja
fast rápido; ~ **food** la comida
   rápida
faster más rápido
fat free sin grasa
father el padre
fax v enviar un fax; ~ n el fax;
   ~ **number** el número de fax
fee la tasa
feed v alimentar

ferry el ferry
fever la fiebre
field (sports) el campo
fill v llenar ; ~ **out** v **(form)**
   rellenar
filling (tooth) el empaste
film (camera) el carrete
fine (fee for breaking law)
   la multa
finger el dedo; **~nail** la uña
   del dedo
fire fuego; ~ **department** los
   bomberos; ~ **door** la puerta
   de incendios
first primero; ~ **class** la
   primera clase
fit (clothing) quedar bien
fitting room el probador
fix v **(repair)** reparar
flashlight la linterna
flight el vuelo
floor el suelo
flower la flor
folk music la música folk
food la comida
foot el pie
football [BE] el fútbol
for para/por
forecast el pronóstico
forest el bosque
fork el tenedor
form el formulario
formula (baby) la fórmula
   infantil
fort el fuerte

fountain la fuente
free gratuito
freezer el congelador
fresh fresco
friend el amigo
frying pan la sartén
full completo; **~-service** el servicio completo; **~-time** a tiempo completo

G

game el partido
garage (parking) el garaje; **~ (repair)** el taller
garbage bag la bolsa de basura
gas la gasolina; **~ station** la gasolinera
gate (airport) la puerta
gay gay; **~ bar** el bar gay; **~ club** la discoteca gay
gel (hair) la gomina
get to v ir a
get off v **(a train/bus/ subway)** bajarse
gift el regalo; **~ shop** la tienda de regalos
girl la niña; **~friend** la novia
give v dar
glass (drinking) el vaso; **~ (material)** el vidrio
glasses las gafas
go v **(somewhere)** ir a
gold el oro
golf golf; **~ course** el campo de golf; **~ tournament** el torneo de golf
good n el producto; ~ adj bueno; **~ afternoon** buenas tardes; **~ evening** buenas noches; **~ morning** buenos días; **~bye** adiós
gram el gramo
grandchild el nieto
grandparent el abuelo
gray gris
green verde
grocery store el supermercado
ground la tierra; **~ floor** la planta baja; **~cloth** la tela impermeable
group el grupo
guide el guía; **~ book** la guía; **~ dog** el perro guía
gym el gimnasio
gynecologist el ginecólogo

H

hair el pelo; **~ dryer** el secador de pelo; **~ salon** la peluquería; **~brush** el cepillo de pelo; **~cut** el corte de pelo; **~spray** la laca; **~style** el peinado; **~stylist** el estilista
half medio; **~ hour** la media hora; **~-kilo** el medio kilo
hammer el martillo
hand la mano; **~ luggage [BE]**

el equipaje de mano; ~bag
[BE] el bolso
handicapped discapacitado;
~-accessible el acceso para
discapacitados
hangover la resaca
happy feliz
hat el sombrero
have v tener
head (body part) la cabeza;
~ache el dolor de cabeza;
~phones los cascos
health la salud; ~ food store
la tienda de alimentos
naturales
heart el corazón; ~ condition
padecer del corazón
heat v calentar; ~ n el calor
heater [heating BE] la
calefacción
hello hola
helmet el casco
help v ayudar; ~ n la ayuda
here aquí
hi hola
high alto; ~chair la trona;
~way la autopista
hiking boots las botas de
montaña
hill la colina
hire v [BE] alquilar; ~ car [BE]
el coche de alquiler
hitchhike v hacer autostop
hockey el hockey
holiday [BE] las vacaciones

horse track el hipódromo
hospital el hospital
hostel el albergue
hot (temperature) caliente;
~ (spicy) picante; ~ spring
el agua termale; ~ water el
agua caliente
hotel el hotel
hour la hora
house la casa; ~hold goods
los artículos para el hogar;
~keeping services el
servicio de limpieza de
habitaciones
how (question) cómo; ~ much
(question) cuánto cuesta
hug v abrazar
hungry hambriento
hurt v (have pain) tener dolor
husband el marido

I

ibuprofen el ibuprofeno
ice el hielo; ~ hockey el
hockey sobre hielo
icy adj helado
identification el documento
de identidad
ill v (to feel) encontrarse mal
in dentro
include v incluir
indoor pool la piscina cubierta
inexpensive barato
infected infectado
information (phone) el

número de teléfono de
información; **~ desk** el
mostrador de información
insect el insecto; **~ bite**
la picadura de insecto;
~ repellent el repelente
de insectos
insert *v* introducir
insomnia el insomnio
instant message el mensaje
instantáneo
insulin la insulina
insurance el seguro; **~ card**
la tarjeta de seguro; **~
company** la compañía de
seguros
interesting interesante
intermediate el nivel
intermedio
international (airport area)
internacional; **~ flight**
el vuelo internacional; **~
student card** la tarjeta
internacional de estudiante
internet la internet; **~ cafe**
el cibercafé; **~ service**
el servicio de internet;
wireless ~ el acceso
inalámbrico
interpreter el/la intérprete
intersection el cruce
intestine el intestino
introduce *v* presentar
invoice [BE] la factura
Ireland Irlanda

Irish irlandés
iron *v* planchar; **~** *n* **(clothes)**
la plancha
Italian italiano

J

jacket la chaqueta
jar el bote
jaw la mandíbula
jazz el jazz; **~ club** el club de
jazz
jeans los vaqueros
jet ski la moto acuática
jeweler la joyería
jewelry las joyas
join *v* acompañar a
joint (body part) la
articulación

K

key la llave; **~ card** la llave
electrónica; **~ ring** el llavero
kiddie pool la piscina infantil
kidney (body part) el riñón
kilo el kilo; **~gram** el
kilogramo; **~meter** el
kilómetro
kiss *v* besar
kitchen la cocina; **~ foil [BE]**
el papel de aluminio
knee la rodilla
knife el cuchillo

L

lace el encaje

lactose intolerant alérgico a la lactosa
lake el lago
large grande; **~er** más grande
last último
late (time) tarde; **~er** más tarde
launderette [BE] la lavandería
laundromat la lavandería
laundry la colada; **~ facility** la lavandería; **~ service** el servicio de lavandería
lawyer el abogado
leather el cuero
to leave v salir
left (direction) la izquierda
leg la pierna
lens la lente
less menos
lesson la lección
letter la carta
library la biblioteca
life la vida; **~ jacket** el chaleco salvavidas; **~guard** el socorrista
lift n **[BE]** el ascensor; **~** v **(to give a ride)** llevar en coche; **~ pass** el pase de acceso a los remontes
light n **(overhead)** la luz; **~** v **(cigarette)** dar fuego; **~bulb** la bombilla
lighter el mechero
like v gustar; **I like** me gusta
line (train) la línea

linen el lino
lip el labio
liquor store la tienda de bebidas alcohólicas
liter el litro
little pequeño
live v vivir
liver (body part) el hígado
loafers los mocasines
local de la zona
lock v cerrar; **~** n el cerrojo
locker la taquilla
log on v **(computer)** iniciar sesión
log off v **(computer)** cerrar sesión
long largo; **~ sleeves** las mangas largas; **~-sighted [BE]** hipermétrope
look v mirar
lose v **(something)** perder
lost perdido; **~ and found** la oficina de objetos perdidos
lotion la crema hidratante
louder más alto
love v querer; **~** n el amor
low bajo; **~er** más bajo
luggage el equipaje; **~ cart** el carrito de equipaje; **~ locker** la consigna automática; **~ ticket** el talón de equipaje; **hand ~ [BE]** el equipaje de mano
lunch la comida
lung el pulmón

M

magazine la revista
magnificent magnífico
mail v enviar por correo; ~
n el correo; ~box el buzón
de correo
main principal; ~ attractions
los principales sitios de
interés; ~ course el plato
principal
make up a prescription v [BE]
despachar medicamentos
mall el centro comercial
man el hombre
manager el gerente
manicure la manicura
manual car el coche con
transmisión manual
map el mapa
market el mercado
married casado
marry v casarse
mass (church service) la misa
massage el masaje
match la cerilla
meal la comida
measure v (someone) medir
measuring cup la taza
medidora
measuring spoon la cuchara
medidora
mechanic el mecánico
medicine el medicamento
medium (size) mediano

meet v (someone) conocer
meeting la reunión; ~ room
la sala de reuniones
membership card la tarjeta
de socio
memorial (place) el
monumento conmemorativo
memory card la tarjeta de
memoria
mend v zurcir
menstrual cramps los dolores
menstruales
menu la carta
message el mensaje
meter (parking) el
parquímetro
microwave el microondas
midday [BE] el mediodía
midnight la medianoche
mileage el kilometraje
mini-bar el minibar
minute el minuto
missing desaparecido
mistake el error
mobile móvil; ~ home
la caravana; ~ phone [BE]
el teléfono móvil
mobility la movilidad
money el dinero
month el mes
mop la fregona
moped el ciclomotor
more más
morning la mañana
mosque la mezquita

mother la madre
motion sickness el mareo
motor el motor; ~ **boat** la lancha motora; ~**cycle** la motocicleta; ~**way [BE]** la autopista
mountain la montaña; ~ **bike** la bicicleta de montaña
mousse (hair) la espuma para el pelo
mouth *n* la boca
movie la película; ~ **theater** el cine
mug *v* asaltar
muscle (body part) el músculo
museum el museo
music la música; ~ **store** la tienda de música

N

nail la uña; ~ **file** la lima de uñas; ~ **salon** el salon de manicura
name el nombre
napkin la servilleta
nappy [BE] el pañale
nationality la nacionalidad
nature preserve la reserva natural
(be) nauseous *v* tener náuseas
near cerca; ~~**sighted** miope; ~**by** cerca de aquí
neck el cuello

necklace el collar
need *v* necesitar
newspaper el periódico
newsstand el quiosco
next próximo
nice *adj* amable
night la noche; ~**club** la discoteca
no no
non sin; ~~**alcoholic** sin alcohol; ~~**smoking** para no fumadores
noon el mediodía
north el norte
nose la nariz
note [BE] el billete
nothing nada
notify *v* avisar
novice (skill level) principiante
now ahora
number el número
nurse el enfermero/la enfermera

O

office la oficina; ~ **hours (doctor's)** las horas de consulta; ~ **hours (other offices)** el horario de oficina
off-licence [BE] la tienda de bebidas alcohólicas
oil el aceite
OK de acuerdo
old *adj* viejo

on the corner en la esquina
once una vez
one uno; **~-way ticket** el
  billete de ida; **~-way street** la
  calle de sentido único
only solamente
open v abrir; ~ adj abierto
opera la ópera; **~ house** el
  teatro de la ópera
opposite frente a
optician el oculista
orange (color) naranja
orchestra la orquesta
order v pedir
outdoor pool la piscina
  exterior
outside fuera
over sobre; **~ the counter**
  (medication) sin receta;
  ~look (scenic place) el
  mirador; **~night** por la noche
oxygen treatment
  la oxígenoterapia

P

p.m. de la tarde
pacifier el chupete
pack v hacer las maletas
package el paquete
paddling pool [BE] la piscina
  infantil
pad [BE] la compresa
pain el dolor
pajamas los pijamas
palace el palacio

pants los pantalones
pantyhose las medias
paper el papel; **~ towel** el
  papel de cocina
paracetamol [BE] el
  paracetamol
park v aparcar; ~ n el parque;
  ~ing garage el párking;
  ~ing lot el aparcamiento
parliament building el palacio
  de las cortes
part (for car) la pieza; **~-time**
  a tiempo parcial
pass through v estar de paso
passenger el pasajero
passport el pasaporte;
  ~ control el control de
  pasaportes
password la contraseña
pastry shop la pastelería
path el camino
pay v pagar; **~ phone** el
  teléfono público
peak (of a mountain) la cima
pearl la perla
pedestrian el peatón
pediatrician el pediatra
pedicure la pedicura
pen el bolígrafo
penicillin la penicilina
penis el pene
per por; **~ day** por día; **~ hour**
  por hora; **~ night** por noche;
  ~ week por semana
perfume el perfume

period (menstrual) la regla;
~ **(of time)** la época
permit v permitir
petite las tallas pequeñas
petrol la gasolina; ~ **station**
la gasolinera
pewter el peltre
pharmacy la farmacia
phone v hacer una llamada;
~ n el teléfono; ~ **call** la
llamada de teléfono; ~
card la tarjeta telefónica;
~ **number** el número de
teléfono
photo la foto; ~**copy** la
fotocopia; ~**graphy** la
fotografía
pick up v **(something)** recoger
picnic area la zona para picnic
piece el trozo
Pill (birth control) la píldora
pillow la almohada
**personal identification
number (PIN)** la clave
pink rosa
piste [BE] la pista; ~ **map [BE]**
el mapa de pistas
pizzeria la pizzería
place v **(a bet)** hacer una
apuesta
plane el avión
plastic wrap el film
transparente
plate el plato
platform [BE] (train) el andén

platinum el platino
play v jugar; ~ n **(theater)**
la obra de teatro; ~**ground**
el patio de recreo; ~**pen** el
parque
please por favor
pleasure el placer
plunger el desatascador
plus size la talla grande
pocket el bolsillo
poison el veneno
poles (skiing) los bastones
police la policía; ~ **report**
el certificado de la policía;
~ **station** la comisaría
pond el estanque
pool la piscina
pop music la música pop
portion la ración
post [BE] el correo; ~ **office**
la oficina de correos; ~**box**
[BE] el buzón de correos;
~**card** la tarjeta postal
pot la olla
pottery la cerámica
pounds (British sterling) las
libras esterlinas
pregnant embarazada
prescribe v recetar
prescription la receta
press v **(clothing)** planchar
price el precio
print v imprimir
problem el problema
produce las frutas y verduras;

~ **store** la frutería y verdulería
prohibit v prohibir
pronounce v pronunciar
public el público
pull v (door sign) tirar
purple morado
purse el bolso
push v (door sign) empujar; ~**chair** [BE] el cochecito de niño

Q

quality n la calidad
question la pregunta
quiet adj tranquilo

R

racetrack el circuito de carreras
racket (sports) la raqueta
railway station [BE] la estación de trenes
rain la lluvia; ~**coat** el chubasquero; ~**forest** el bosque pluvial; ~**y** adv lluvioso
rap (music) el rap
rape v violar; ~ n la violación
rash la erupción cutánea
razor blade la hoja de afeitar
reach v localizar
ready listo
real auténtico
receipt el recibo

receive v recibir
reception la recepción
recharge v recargar
recommend v recomendar
recommendation la recomendación
recycle v reciclar
red rojo
refrigerator n la nevera
region la región
registered mail el correo certificado
regular normal
relationship la relación
rent v alquilar
rental car el coche de alquiler
repair v arreglar
repeat v repetir
reservation la reserva; ~ **desk** la taquilla
reserve v reservar
restaurant el restaurante
restroom el servicio
retired jubilado
return v (something) devolver; ~ n [BE] la ida y vuelta
rib (body part) la costilla
right (direction) derecha; ~ **of way** prioridad de paso
ring el anillo
river n el río
road map el mapa de carreteras
rob v atracar
robbed atracado

romantic romántico
room la habitación; ~ **key** la llave de habitación; ~ **service** el servicio de habitaciones
round-trip ida y vuelta
route la ruta
rowboat la barca de remos
rubbish [BE] la basura; ~ **bag** [BE] la bolsa de basura
rugby el rugby
ruins las ruinas
rush la prisa

S

sad triste
safe n la caja fuerte; ~ adj seguro
sales tax el IVA
same mismo
sandals las sandalias
sanitary napkin la compresa
saucepan el cazo
sauna la sauna
save v (computer) guardar
savings (account) la cuenta de ahorro
scanner el escáner
scarf la bufanda
schedule v programar; ~ n el horario
school el colegio
science la ciencia
scissors las tijeras
sea el mar
seat el asiento

security la seguridad
see v ver
self-service el autoservicio
sell v vender
seminar el seminario
send v enviar
senior citizen jubilado
separated (marriage) -separado
serious serio
service (in a restaurant) el servicio
sexually transmitted disease (STD) la enfermedad de transmisión sexual
shampoo el champú
sharp afilado
shaving cream la crema de afeitar
sheet la sábana
ship v enviar
shirt la camisa
shoe store la zapatería
shoes los zapatos
shop v comprar
shopping ir de compras; ~ **area** la zona de compras; ~ **centre** [BE] el centro comercial; ~ **mall** el centro comercial
short corto; ~ **sleeves** las mangas cortas; ~**s** los pantalones cortos; ~**-sighted** [BE] miope
shoulder el hombro

show v enseñar
shower la ducha
shrine el santuario
sick enfermo
side el lado; **~ dish** la guarnición; **~ effect** el efecto secundario; **~ order** la guarnición
sightsee v hacer turismo
sightseeing tour el recorrido turístico
sign v (name) firmar
silk la seda
silver la plata
single (unmarried) soltero; **~ bed** la cama; **~ prints** una copia; **~ room** una habitación individual
sink el lavabo
sister la hermana
sit v sentarse
size la talla
skin la piel
skirt la falda
ski v esquiar; **~** n el esquí; **~ lift** el telesquí
sleep v dormir; **~er car** el coche cama; **~ing bag** el saco de dormir
slice v cortar en rodajas
slippers las zapatillas
slower más despacio
slowly despacio
small pequeño
smaller más pequeño

smoke v fumar
smoking (area) la zona de fumadores
snack bar la cafetería
sneakers las zapatillas de deporte
snorkeling equipment el equipo de esnórquel
snow la nieve; **~board** la tabla de snowboard; **~shoe** la raqueta de nieve; **~y** nevado
soap el jabón
soccer el fútbol
sock el calcetín
some alguno
soother [BE] el chupete
sore throat las anginas
sorry lo siento
south el sur
souvenir el recuerdo; **~ store** la tienda de recuerdos
spa el centro de salud y belleza
Spain España
Spanish el español
spatula la espátula
speak v hablar
special (food) la especialidad de la casa
specialist (doctor) el especialista
specimen el ejemplar
speeding el exceso de velocidad
spell v deletrear

spicy picante

spine (body part) la columna vertebral

spoon la cuchara

sports los deportes; ~ massage el masaje deportivo

sporting goods store la tienda de deportes

sprain el esguince

square cuadrado; ~ kilometer el kilómetro cuadrado; ~ meter el metro cuadrado

stadium el estadio

stairs las escaleras

stamp v (a ticket) picar; ~ n (postage) el sello

start v empezar

starter [BE] el aperitivo

station la estación; bus ~ la estación de autobuses; gas ~ la gasolinera; muster ~ [BE] el punto de reunión; petrol ~ [BE] la gasolinera; subway ~ el metro; train ~ la estación de tren

statue la estatua

stay v quedarse

steal v robar

steep empinado

sterling silver la plata esterlina

sting el escozor

stolen robado

stomach el estómago; ~ache el dolor de estómago

stop v pararse; ~ n la parada

storey [BE] la planta

stove el horno

straight recto

strange extraño

stream el arroyo

stroller el cochecito

student el estudiante

study v estudiar

stunning impresionante

subtitle el subtítulo

subway el metro; ~ station la estación de metro

suit el traje

suitcase la maleta

sun el sol; ~block el protector solar total; ~burn la quemadura solar; ~glasses las gafas de sol; ~ny soleado; ~screen el protector solar; ~stroke la insolación

super (fuel) súper; ~market el supermercado

surfboard la tabla de surf

surgical spirit [BE] el alcohol etílico

swallow v tragar

sweater el jersey

sweatshirt la sudadera

sweet (taste) dulce; ~s [BE] los caramelos

swelling la hinchazón

swim v nadar; ~suit el bañador

symbol (keyboard) el símbolo
synagogue la sinagoga

T

table la mesa
tablet (medicine) el comprimido
take v llevar; **~ away [BE]** para llevar
tampon el tampón
tapas bar el bar de tapas
taste v probar
taxi el taxi
team el equipo
telephone el teléfono
temporary provisional
tennis el tenis
tent la tienda de campaña; **~ peg** la estaca; **~ pole** el mástil
terminal (airport) la terminal
terracotta la terracotta
terrible terrible
text v **(send a message)** enviar un mensaje de texto; **~** n **(message)** el texto
thank v dar las gracias a; **~ you** gracias
that eso
theater el teatro
there ahí
thief el ladrón
thigh el muslo
thirsty sediento
this esto

throat la garganta
ticket el billete; **~ office** el despacho de billetes; **~ed passenger** el pasajero con billete
tie (clothing) la corbata
time el tiempo; **~table [BE]** el horario
tire la rueda
tired cansado
tissue el pañuelo de paper
tobacconist el estanco
today hoy
toe el dedo del pie; **~nail** la uña del pie
toilet [BE] el servicio; **~ paper** el papel higiénico
tomorrow mañana
tongue la lengua
tonight esta noche
too demasiado
tooth el diente; **~brush** el cepillo de dientes; **~paste** la pasta de dientes
total (amount) el total
tough (food) duro
tourist el turista; **~ information office** la oficina de turismo
tour el recorrido turístico
tow truck la grúa
towel la toalla
tower la torre
town la ciudad; **~ hall** el ayuntamiento; **~ map** el

mapa de ciudad; **~ square** la plaza

toy el juguete; **~ store** la tienda de juguetes

track (train) el andén

traditional tradicional

traffic light el semáforo

trail la pista; **~ map** el mapa de la pista

trailer el remolque

train el tren; **~ station** la estación de tren

transfer v cambiar

translate v traducir

trash la basura

travel v viajar; **~ agency** la agencia de viajes; **~ sickness** el mareo; **~er's check [cheque BE]** el cheque de viaje

tree el árbol

trim (hair cut) cortarse las puntas

trip el viaje

trolley [BE] el carrito

trousers [BE] los pantalones

T-shirt la camiseta

turn off v apagar

turn on v encender

TV la televisión

type v escribir a máquina

tyre [BE] la rueda

U

United Kingdom (U.K.) el Reino Unido

United States (U.S.) los Estados Unidos

ugly feo

umbrella el paraguas

unattended desatendido

unconscious inconsciente

underground [BE] el metro; **~ station [BE]** la estación de metro

underpants [BE] los calzoncillos

understand v entender

underwear la ropa interior

university la universidad

unleaded (gas) la gasolina sin plomo

upper superior

urgent urgente

use v usar

username el nombre de usuario

utensil el cubierto

V

vacancy la habitación libre

vacation las vacaciones

vaccination la vacuna

vacuum cleaner la aspiradora

vaginal infection la infección vaginal

valid validez

valley el valle

valuable valioso

VAT [BE] el IVA

vegetarian vegetariano

vehicle registration el registro del coche

viewpoint [BE] el mirador

village el pueblo

vineyard la viña

visa (passport document) el visado

visit v visitar; **~ing hours** el horario de visita

visually impaired la persona con discapacidad visual

vitamin la vitamina

V-neck el cuello de pico

vomit v vomitar

W

wait v esperar; **~** n la espera; **~ing room** la sala de espera

waiter el camarero

waitress la camarera

wake v despertarse; **~-up call** la llamada despertador

walk v caminar; **~** n la caminata; **~ing route** la ruta de senderismo

wallet la cartera

warm v (something) calentar; **~** adj (temperature) calor

washing machine la lavadora

watch el reloj

waterfall la cascada

weather el tiempo

week la semana; **~end** el fin de semana; **~ly** semanal

welcome v acoger

well bien; **~-rested** descansado

west el oeste

what (question) qué

wheelchair la silla de ruedas; **~ ramp** la rampa para silla de ruedas

when (question) cuándo

where (question) dónde

white blanco; **~ gold** el oro blanco

who (question) quién

widowed viudo

wife la mujer

window la ventana; **~ case** el escaparate

windsurfer el surfista

wine list la carta de vinos

wireless inalámbrico; **~ internet** el acceso inalámbrico a internet; **~ internet service** el servicio inalámbrico a internet; **~ phone** el teléfono móvil

with con

withdraw v retirar; **~al (bank)** retirar fondos

without sin

woman la mujer

wool la lana

work v trabajar

wrap v envolver

wrist la muñeca

write v escribir

Y

year el año
yellow amarillo
yes sí
yesterday ayer

young joven
youth hostel el albergue
  juvenil

Z

zoo el zoológico

SPANISH–ENGLISH

A

a tiempo completo full-time
a tiempo parcial part-time
la abadía abbey
el abanico fan (souvenir)
abierto *adj* open
el abogado lawyer
abrazar *v* hug
el abrebotellas bottle opener
el abrelatas can opener
el abrigo coat
abrir *v* open
el abuelo grandparent
aburrido boring
acampar *v* camp
el acantilado cliff
el acceso access;
  ~ inalámbrico a internet
  wireless internet; **~ para**
  discapacitados
  handicapped-
  [disabled- BE] accessible
el accidente accident
el aceite oil

aceptar *v* accept
acoger *v* welcome
acompañar a *v* join
la acupuntura acupuncture
el adaptador adapter
adicional extra
adiós goodbye
las aduanas customs
el aeropuerto airport
afilado sharp
la agencia agency; **~ de**
  viajes travel agency
agotado exhausted
el agua water; **~ caliente**
  hot water; **~ potable**
  drinking water
las aguas termales hot spring
ahí there
ahora now
el aire air, air pump;
  ~ acondicionado
  air conditioning
el albergue hostel; **~ juvenil**
  youth hostel

alérgico allergic;
~ **a la lactosa** lactose intolerant
algo anything
el algodón cotton
alguno some
alimentar v feed
el allanamiento de morada break-in (burglary)
la almohada pillow
el alojamiento accommodation
alquilar v rent [hire BE];
el ~ de coches car rental [hire BE]
alto high
amable nice
amarillo yellow
la ambulancia ambulance
el amigo friend
el amor n love
el andén track [platform BE] (train)
anémico anemic
la anestesia anesthesia
las anginas sore throat
el anillo ring
el animal animal
antes de before
el antibiótico antibiotic
el año year
apagar v turn off
el aparcamiento parking lot [car park BE]
aparcar v park

el apartamento apartment
el apéndice appendix (body part)
el aperitivo appetizer [starter BE]
aquí here
el árbol tree
la aromaterapia aromatherapy
arreglar v repair
el arroyo stream
la arteria artery
la articulación joint (body part)
los artículos goods; ~ **para el hogar** household good
la artritis arthritis
asaltar v mug
el asalto attack
el ascensor elevator [lift BE]
asiático Asian
el asiento seat; ~ **de niño** car seat; ~ **de pasillo** aisle seat
asistir v attend
asmático asthmatic
la aspiradora vacuum cleaner
la aspirina aspirin
atracado robbed
atracar v rob
Australia Australia
australiano Australian
auténtico real
el autobús bus; ~ **rápido** express bus
automático automatic

la autopista highway [motorway BE]

el autoservicio self-service

la avería breakdown

el avión airplane, plane

avisar *v* notify

ayer yesterday

la ayuda *n* help

ayudar *v* help

el ayuntamiento town hall

azul blue

B

bailar *v* dance

bajarse *v* get off (a train, bus, subway)

bajo low

el ballet ballet

el baloncesto basketball

el bálsamo para después del afeitado aftershave

el banco bank

el bañador swimsuit

el baño bathroom

el bar bar; ~ **de tapas** tapas bar; ~ **gay** gay bar

barato cheap, inexpensive

la barbacoa barbecue

la barca de remos rowboat

el barco boat

los bastones poles (skiing)

la basura trash [rubbish BE]

la batería battery (car)

el bebé baby

beber *v* drink

la bebida *n* drink

beis beige

el béisbol baseball

besar *v* kiss

el biberón baby bottle

la biblioteca library

la bicicleta bicycle; ~ **de montaña** mountain bike

el billete *n* bill (money); ~ ticket; ~ **de autobús** bus ticket; ~ **de ida** one-way (ticket); ~ **de ida y vuelta** round trip [return BE]; ~ **electrónico** e-ticket

el biquini bikini

blanco white

la blusa blouse

la boca mouth

el bolígrafo pen

la bolsa de basura garbage [rubbish BE] bag

el bolsillo pocket

el bolso purse [handbag BE]

los bomberos fire department

la bombilla lightbulb

borrar *v* clear (on an ATM); ~ *v* delete (computer)

el bosque forest; ~ **pluvial** rainforest

las botas boots; ~ **de montaña** hiking boots

el bote jar

la botella bottle

el brazo arm

británico British
el broche brooch
bucear to dive
bueno *adj* good
buenas noches good evening
buenas tardes good afternoon
buenos días good morning
la bufanda scarf
el buzón de correo mailbox [postbox BE]

C

la cabaña cabin (house)
el cabaré cabaret
la cabeza head (body part)
la cafetería cafe, coffee shop, snack bar
la caja case (amount); **~ fuerte** *n* safe
el cajero cashier; **~ automático** ATM
el calcetín sock
la calefacción heater [heating BE]
calentar *v* heat, warm
la calidad quality
la calle de sentido único one-way street
calor hot, warm (temperature)
las calorías calories
los calzoncillos briefs [underpants BE] (clothing)
la cama single bed; **~ de matrimonio** double bed

la cámara camera; **~ digital** digital camera
la camarera waitress
el camarero waiter
el camarote cabin (ship)
cambiar *v* change, exchange, transfer
el cambio *n* change (money); **~ de divisas** currency exchange
caminar *v* walk
la caminata *n* walk
el camino path
la camisa shirt
la camiseta T-shirt
el cámping campsite
el campo field (sports); **~ de batalla** battleground; **~ de golf** golf course
Canadá Canada
canadiense Canadian
cancelar *v* cancel
el/la canguro babysitter
cansado tired
el cañón canyon
la cara face
los caramelos candy [sweets BE]
la caravana mobile home
el carbón charcoal
el carnicero butcher
caro expensive
el carrete film (camera)
el carrito cart [trolley BE] (grocery store); **~ de equipaje**

luggage cart
la **carta** letter
la **carta** n menu; ~ **de bebidas** drink menu; ~ **para niños** children's menu; ~ **de vinos** wine list
la **cartera** n wallet
el **cartón** carton; ~ **de tabaco** carton of cigarettes
la **casa** house; ~ **de cambio** currency exchange office
casado married
casarse v marry
la **cascada** waterfall
el **casco** helmet
los **cascos** headphones
el **casino** casino
el **castillo** castle
el **catarro** cold (sickness)
la **catedral** cathedral
el **catre** cot
causar daño v damage
el **cazo** saucepan
el **CD** CD
la **cena** dinner
el **centímetro** centimeter
el **centro** downtown area; ~ **comercial** shopping mall [centre BE]; ~ **de negocios** business center; ~ **de salud y belleza** spa
el **cepillo de pelo** hair brush
la **cerámica** pottery
cerca near; ~ **de aquí** nearby
la **cerilla** n match

cerrado closed
cerrar v close, lock; ~ **sesión** v log off (computer)
el **cerrojo** n lock
el **certificado** certificate; ~ **de la policía** police report
la **cesta** basket (grocery store)
el **chaleco salvavidas** life jacket
el **champú** shampoo
la **chaqueta** jacket
la **charcutería** delicatessen
el **cheque** n check [cheque BE] (payment); ~ **de viaje** traveler's check [cheque BE]
el **chicle** chewing gum
chino Chinese
el **chubasquero** raincoat
el **chupete** pacifier [soother BE]
el **cibercafé** internet cafe
el **ciclismo** cycling
el **ciclomotor** moped
la **ciencia** science
el **cigarrillo** cigarette
la **cima** peak (of a mountain)
el **cine** movie theater
la **cinta transportadora** conveyor belt
el **cinturón** n belt
el **circuito de carreras** racetrack
la **cita** appointment
la **ciudad** town

la clase class; **~ económica** economy class; **~ preferente** business class

la clave personal identification number (PIN)

el club de jazz jazz club

cobrar v bill (charge); **~** v cash; **~** v charge (credit card)

el cobre copper

el coche n car; **~ de alquiler** rental [hire BE] car; **~ automático** automatic car; **~ cama** sleeper [sleeping BE] car; **~ con transmisión manual** manual car

el cochecito stroller [pushchair BE]

la cocina kitchen

cocinar v cook

el código de país country code

el codo elbow

la colada laundry

el colegio school

la colina hill

el collar necklace

la colonia cologne

el color color

la columna vertebral spine (body part)

el comedor dining room

comer v eat

la comida food, lunch, meal; **~ rápida** fast food

la comisaría police station

cómo how

el compañero de trabajo colleague

la compañia company; **~ aérea** airline; **~ de seguros** insurance company

comprar v buy, shop

la compresa sanitary napkin [pad BE]

el comprimido tablet (medicine)

con with; **~ plomo** leaded (gas)

el concierto concert

conducir v drive

conectarse v connect (internet)

la conexión connection (internet); **~ de vuelo** connection (flight)

la conferencia conference

confirmar v confirm

el congelador freezer

la congestión congestion

conocer v meet (someone)

la consigna automática luggage locker

el consulado Consulate

el consultor consultant

contagioso contagious

la contraseña password

el control de pasaportes passport control

el corazón heart

la corbata tie (clothing)

el correo n mail [post

BE]; **~ aéreo** airmail; **~ certificado** registered mail; **~ electrónico** *n* e-mail

cortar *v* cut (hair); **~ en rodajas** to slice

cortarse las puntas *v* trim (hair cut)

el corte *n* cut (injury); **~ de pelo** haircut

corto short

costar *v* cost

la costilla rib (body part)

la crema cream; **~ antiséptica** antiseptic cream; **~ de afeitar** shaving cream; **~ hidratante** lotion

el cristal crystal

el cruce intersection

cuándo when (question)

cuánto cuesta how much

el cubierto utensil

la cuchara spoon; **~ medidora** measuring spoon

la cucharadita teaspoon

la cuchilla desechable disposable razor

el cuchillo knife

el cuello neck; **~ de pico** V-neck; **~ redondo** crew neck

el cuenco bowl

la cuenta account; **~ de ahorro** savings account; **~ corriente** checking [current BE] account

cuero leather

la cueva cave

el cumpleaños birthday

la cuna crib

D

dar to give; **~ el pecho** breastfeed; **~ fuego** light (cigarette); **~ las gracias a** *v* thank

de from, of; **~ acuerdo** OK; **~ la mañana** a.m.; **~ la tarde** p.m.; **~ la zona** local

declarar *v* declare

el dedo finger; **~ del pie** toe

deletrear *v* spell

delicioso delicious

la dentadura denture

el dentista dentist

dentro in

la depilacion wax; **~ de cejas** eyebrow wax; **~ de las ingles** bikini wax

deportes sports

depositar *v* deposit

el depósito bancario deposit (bank)

la derecha right (direction)

desaparecido missing

el desatascador plunger

desatendido unattended

el desayuno breakfast

descansado well-rested

desconectar *v* disconnect (computer)

el descuento discount

desechable disposable
el desierto desert
el desodorante deodorant
despachar medicamentos v fill [make up BE] a prescription
el despacho de billetes ticket office
despacio slowly
despertarse v wake
después after
el detergente detergent
detrás de behind (direction)
devolver v exchange, return (goods)
el día day
diabético diabetic
el diamante diamond
la diarrea diarrhea
el diente tooth
el diesel diesel
difícil difficult
digital digital
el dinero money
la dirección direction
la dirección address; **~ de correo electrónico** e-mail address
discapacitado handicapped [disabled BE]
la discoteca club (dance, night); **~ gay** gay club
disculparse v excuse (to get attention)
disfrutar v enjoy

disponible available
divorciar v divorce
doblada dubbed
doblando (la esquina) around (the corner)
la docena dozen
el documento de identidad identification
el dólar dollar (U.S.)
el dolor pain; **~ de cabeza** headache; **~ de espalda** backache; **~ de estómago** stomachache; **~ de oído** earache; **~ de pecho** chest pain
los dolores menstruales menstrual cramps
dónde where (question)
dormir v sleep
el dormitorio dormitory
la ducha shower
dulce sweet (taste)
durante during
el DVD DVD

E

la edad age
el edificio building
el efectivo cash
el efecto secundario side effect
el ejemplar specimen
embarazada pregnant
embarcar v board
la emergencia emergency

el empaste filling (tooth)
empezar v begin, start
empinado steep
empujar v push (door sign)
en la esquina on the corner
el encaje lace
encender v turn on
el enchufe eléctrico electric outlet
encontrarse mal v be ill
la enfermedad de transmisión sexual sexually transmitted disease (STD)
el enfermero/la enfermera nurse
enfermo sick
enseñar v show
entender v understand
la entrada admission/cover charge; ~ entrance
entrar v enter
el entretenimiento entertainment
enviar v send, ship; ~ **por correo** v mail; ~ **un correo electrónico** v e-mail; ~ **un fax** v fax ; ~ **un mensaje de texto** v text (send a message)
envolver v wrap
la época period (of time)
el equipaje luggage [baggage BE]; ~ **de mano** carry-on (piece of hand luggage)
el equipo team

el equipo equipment; ~ **de buceo** diving equipment; ~ **de esnórquel** snorkeling equipment
equis ele (XL) extra large
el error mistake
la erupción cutánea rash
las escaleras stairs; ~ **mecánicas** escalators
el escáner scanner
el escaparate window case
la escoba broom
el escozor sting
escribir v write; ~ **a máquina** v type
el escurridor colander
el esguince sprain
el esmalte enamel (jewelry)
eso that
la espalda back
España Spain
el español Spanish
la espátula spatula
la especialidad de la casa special (food)
el especialista specialist (doctor)
la espera n wait
esperar v wait
la espuma para el pelo mousse (hair)
el esquí n ski
esquiar v ski
los esquís acuáticos water skis

esta noche tonight
la estaca tent peg
la estación station;
~ **de autobuses** bus station;
~ **de metro** subway
[underground BE] station;
~ **de tren** train [railway BE]
station
el estadio stadium
el estado de salud condition
(medical)
los Estados Unidos United
States (U.S.)
estadounidense American
el estanco tobacconist
el estanque pond
estar v be; ~ **de paso** v pass
through
la estatua statue
el este east
el estilista hairstylist
esto this
el estómago stomach
estrellarse v crash (car)
estreñido constipated
estudiando studying
el estudiante student
estudiar v study
el euro euro
el exceso excess; ~ **de
velocidad** speeding
la excursión excursion
experto expert (skill level)
la extensión extension
(phone)

extraer v extract (tooth)
extraño strange

F

fácil adj easy
la factura bill [invoice BE]
la facturación check-in
(airport)
facturar check (luggage)
la falda skirt
la familia family
la farmacia pharmacy
[chemist BE]
el fax n fax
la fecha date (calendar)
feliz adj happy
feo adj ugly
el ferry ferry
la fianza deposit (to reserve
a room)
la fiebre fever
el film transparente plastic
wrap [cling film BE]
el fin de semana weekend
firmar v sign (name)
la flor flower
la fórmula infantil formula
(baby)
el formulario form
la foto exposure (film);
~ photo; ~**copia** photocopy;
~**grafía** photography;
~ **digital** digital photo
la fregona mop
los frenos brakes (car)

frente a opposite
fresco fresh
frío *adj* cold (temperature)
las frutas y verduras produce
la frutería y verdulería
  produce store
el fuego fire
la fuente fountain
fuera outside
el fuerte fort
fumar *v* smoke
la funda para la cámara
  camera case
el fútbol soccer [football BE]

G

las gafas glasses; **~ de sol**
  sunglasses
el garaje garage (parking)
la garganta throat
la garrafa carafe
el gas butano cooking gas
la gasolina gas [petrol BE];
  ~ sin plomo unleaded gas
la gasolinera gas [petrol BE]
  station
gay gay
el gerente manager
el gimnasio gym
el ginecólogo gynecologist
la gomina gel (hair)
la gota drop (medicine)
grabar *v* burn (CD); **~** *v* engrave
gracias thank you
los grados degrees

(temperature); **~ centígrado**
  Celsius
el gramo gram
grande large
los grandes almacenes
  department store
la granja farm
gratuito free
gris gray
la grúa tow truck
el grupo group
guapo attractive
guardar *v* save (computer)
la guarnición side dish, order
el guía guide
la guía guide book; **~ de**
  tiendas store directory
gustar *v* like; **me gusta** I like

H

ha sufrido daños damaged
la habitación room;
  ~ individual single room;
  ~ libre vacancy
hablar *v* speak
hacer *v* have; **~ una apuesta**
  v place (a bet); **~ un arreglo**
  v alter; **~ una llamada**
  v phone; **~ las maletas** *v*
  pack; **~ turismo** sightseeing
hambriento hungry
helado icy
la hermana sister
el hermano brother
el hielo ice

el hígado liver (body part)
la hinchazón swelling
hipermétrope far-sighted
  [long-sighted BE]
el hipódromo horsetrack
el hockey hockey; **~ sobre**
  hielo ice hockey
la hoja de afeitar razor blade
hola hello
el hombre man
el hombro shoulder
hondo deeply
la hora hour
el horario *n* schedule
  [timetable BE]
los horarios hours; **~ de**
  atención al público
  business hours; **~ de oficina**
  office hours; **~ de visita**
  visiting hours
las horas de consulta office
  hours (doctor's)
el hornillo camp stove
el horno stove
el hospital hospital
el hotel hotel
hoy today
el hueso bone

I

el ibuprofeno ibuprofen
la ida y vuelta round-trip
  [return BE]
la iglesia church
impresionante stunning

imprimir *v* print
el impuesto duty (tax)
incluir *v* include
inconsciente unconscious
increíble amazing
la infección vaginal vaginal
  infection
infectado infected
el inglés English
iniciar sesión *v* log on
  (computer)
el insecto bug
la insolación sunstroke
el insomnio insomnia
la insulina insulin
interesante interesting
internacional international
  (airport area)
la internet internet
el/la intérprete interpreter
el intestino intestine
introducir *v* insert
ir a *v* go (somewhere)
ir de compras *v* go shopping
Irlanda Ireland
irlandés Irish
el IVA sales tax [VAT BE]
la izquierda left (direction)

J

el jabón soap
el jardín botánico
  botanical garden
el jazz jazz
el jersey sweater

joven young
las joyas jewelry
la joyería jeweler
jubilado retired
jugar v play
el juguete toy

K

el kilo kilo; ~**gramo** kilogram;
~**metraje** mileage
el kilómetro kilometer;
~ **cuadrado** square kilometer

L

el labio lip
la laca hairspray
el ladrón thief
el lago lake
la lana wool
la lancha motora motor boat
largo long
el lavabo sink
la lavadora washing machine
la lavandería laundromat
[launderette BE]
lavar v wash
el lavavajillas dishwasher
la lección lesson
lejos far
la lengua tongue
la lente lens
las lentillas de contacto
contact lens
las letras arts
las libras esterlinas pounds

(British sterling)
libre de impuestos duty-free
la librería bookstore
el libro book
la lima de uñas nail file
limpiar v clean
la limpieza de cutis facial
limpio adj clean
la línea line (train)
el lino linen
la linterna flashlight
el líquido liquid; ~ **de lentillas
de contacto** contact lens
solution; ~ **lavavajillas**
dishwashing liquid
listo ready
la litera berth
el litro liter
la llamada n call; ~ **de
teléfono** phone call; ~
despertador wake-up call
llamar v call
la llave key; ~ **de habitación**
room key; ~ **electrónica** key
card
el llavero key ring
las llegadas arrivals (airport)
llegar v arrive
llenar v fill
llevar v take; ~ **en coche** lift
(to give a ride)
la lluvia rain
lluvioso rainy
lo siento sorry
localizar v reach

la luz light (overhead)

M

la madre mother

magnífico magnificent

el malestar estomacal upset stomach

la maleta bag, suitcase

la mandíbula jaw

las mangas cortas short sleeves

las mangas largas long sleeves

la manicura manicure

la mano hand

la manta blanket

mañana tomorrow; **la ~** morning

el mapa map; **~ de carreteras** road map; **~ de ciudad** town map; **~ de la pista** trail [piste BE] map

el mar sea

marcar v dial

mareado dizzy

el mareo motion [travel BE] sickness

el marido husband

marrón brown

el martillo hammer

más more; **~ alto** louder; **~ bajo** lower; **~ barato** cheaper; **~ despacio** slower; **~ grande** larger; **~ pequeño** smaller; **~ rápido** faster;

~ tarde later; **~ temprano** earlier

el masaje massage; **~ deportivo** sports massage

el mástil tent pole

el mecánico mechanic

el mechero lighter

la media hora half hour

mediano medium (size)

la medianoche midnight

el medicamento medicine

el médico doctor

medio half; **~ kilo** half-kilo; **~día** noon [midday BE]

medir v measure (someone)

mejor best

menos less

el mensaje message; **~ instantáneo** instant message

el mercado market

el mes month

la mesa table

el metro subway [underground BE]

el metro cuadrado square meter

la mezquita mosque

el microondas microwave

el minibar mini-bar

el minuto minute

el mirador overlook [viewpoint BE] (scenic place)

mirar v look

la misa mass (church service)

mismo same
los mocasines loafers
la mochila backpack
molestar *v* bother
la moneda coin, currency
mono cute
la montaña *n* mountain
el monumento conmemorativo memorial (place)
morado purple
el mostrador de información information desk
mostrar *v* display
la moto acuática jet ski
la motocicleta motorcycle
movilidad mobility
la mujer wife, woman
la multa fine (fee for breaking law)
la muñeca doll; ~ wrist
el músculo muscle
el museo museum
la música music; ~ **clásica** classical music; ~ **folk** folk music; ~ **pop** pop music
el muslo thigh

N

nacional domestic
la nacionalidad nationality
nada nothing
nadar *v* swim
las nalgas buttocks
naranja orange (color)

la nariz nose
necesitar *v* need
los negocios business
negro black
nevado snowy
la nevera refrigerator
el nieto grandchild
la niña girl
el niño boy, child
el nivel intermedio intermediate
no no
la noche evening, night
el nombre name; ~ **de usuario** username
normal regular
las normas de vestuario dress code
el norte north
la novia girlfriend
el novio boyfriend
el número number; ~ **de fax** fax number; ~ **de permiso de conducir** driver's license number; ~ **de teléfono** phone number; ~ **de teléfono de información** information (phone)

O

la obra de teatro *n* play (theater)
el oculista optician
el oeste west
la oficina office; ~ **de correos**

post office; **~ de objetos
perdidos** lost and found;
~ de turismo tourist
information office

el ojo eye

la olla pot

la ópera opera

el ordenador computer

la oreja ear

la orina urine

el oro gold; **~ amarillo** yellow
gold; **~ blanco** white gold

la orquesta orchestra

oscuro dark

el otro camino alternate route

la oxigenoterapia oxygen
treatment

P

padecer del corazón heart
condition

el padre father

pagar *v* pay

el pájaro bird

el palacio palace; **~ de las
cortes** parliament building

los palillos chinos chopsticks

la panadería bakery

los pantalones pants
[trousers BE]; **~ cortos** shorts

el pañal diaper [nappy BE]

el pañuelo de paper tissue

el papel paper; **~ de aluminio**
aluminum [kitchen BE] foil;
~ de cocina paper towel;

~ higiénico toilet paper

el paquete package

para for; **~ llevar** to go [take
away BE]; **~ no fumadores**
non-smoking

el paracetamol
acetaminophen [paracetamol
BE]

la parada *n* stop;
~ de autobús bus stop

el paraguas umbrella

pararse *v* stop

el párking parking garage

el parque playpen; **~** park; **~
de atracciones** amusement
park

el partido game; **~ de fútbol**
soccer [football BE]; **~ de
voleibol** volleyball game

el pasajero passenger;
~ con billete ticketed
passenger

el pasaporte passport

**el pase de acceso a los
remontes** lift pass

el pasillo aisle

la pasta de dientes
toothpaste

la pastelería pastry shop

el patio de recreo playground

el peatón pedestrian

el pecho chest (body part)

el pediatra pediatrician

la pedicura pedicure

pedir *v* order

el peinado hairstyle
el peine comb
la película movie
peligroso dangerous
el pelo hair
el peltre pewter
la peluquería de caballeros barber
la peluquería hair salon
los pendientes earrings
el pene penis
la penicilina penicillin
la pensión bed and breakfast
pequeño small
perder v lose (something)
perdido lost
el perfume perfume
el periódico newspaper
la perla pearl
permitir v allow, permit
el perro guía guide dog
la persona con discapacidad visual visually impaired person
la picadura de insecto insect bite
picante spicy
picar v stamp (a ticket)
el pie foot
la piel skin
la pierna leg
la pieza part (for car)
los pijamas pajamas
la pila battery
la píldora Pill (birth control)

la piscina pool; ~ cubierta indoor pool; ~ exterior outdoor pool; ~ infantil kiddie [paddling BE] pool
la pista trail [piste BE]
la pizzería pizzeria
el placer pleasure
la plancha n iron (clothes)
planchar v iron
la planta floor [storey BE]; ~ baja ground floor
la plata silver; ~ esterlina sterling silver
el platino platinum
el plato dish (kitchen); ~ principal main course
la playa beach
la plaza town square
la policía police
la pomada cream (ointment)
ponerse en contacto con v contact
por for; ~ per; ~ día per day; ~ favor please; ~ hora per hour; ~ la noche overnight; ~ noche per night; ~ semana per week
el postre dessert
el precio price
precioso beautiful
el prefijo area code
la pregunta question
presentar v introduce
el preservativo condom
la primera clase first class

primero first
los principales sitios de interés main attraction
principiante beginner, novice (skill level)
la prioridad de paso right of way
la prisa rush
el probador fitting room
probar *v* taste
el problema problem
el producto good; **~ de limpieza** cleaning product
programar *v* schedule
prohibir *v* prohibit
el pronóstico forecast
pronunciar *v* pronounce
el protector solar sunscreen
provisional temporary
próximo next
el público public
el pueblo village
el puente bridge
la puerta gate (airport); **~ door; ~ de incendios** fire door
el pulmón lung
la pulsera bracelet
el puro cigar

Q

qué what (question)
quedar bien *v* fit (clothing)
quedarse *v* stay
la queja complaint

la quemadura solar sunburn
querer *v* love (someone)
quién who (question)
el quiosco newsstand

R

la ración portion; **~ para niños** children's portion
la rampa para silla de ruedas wheelchair ramp
el rap rap (music)
rápido express, fast
la raqueta racket (sports); **~ de nieve** snowshoe
la reacción alérgica allergic reaction
recargar *v* recharge
la recepción reception
la receta prescription
recetar *v* prescribe
rechazar *v* decline (credit card)
recibir *v* receive
el recibo receipt
reciclar recycling
recoger *v* pick up (something)
la recogida de equipajes baggage claim
la recomendación recommendation
recomendar *v* recommend
el recorrido tour; **~ en autobús** bus tour; **~ turístico** sightseeing tour
recto straight
el recuerdo souvenir

el regalo gift
la región region
el registro check-in (hotel);
~ **del coche** vehicle
registration
la regla period (menstrual)
el Reino Unido United
Kingdom (U.K.)
la relación relationship
rellenar v fill out (form)
el reloj watch; ~ **de pared** wall
clock
el remolque trailer
reparar v fix (repair)
el repelente de insectos
insect repellent
repetir v repeat
la resaca hangover
la reserva reservation;
~ **natural** nature preserve
reservar v reserve
el/la residente de la UE
EU resident
respirar v breathe
el restaurante restaurant
retirar v withdraw; ~ **fondos**
withdrawal (bank)
retrasarse v delay
la reunión meeting
revelar v develop (film)
revisar v check (on something)
la revista magazine
el riñón kidney (body part)
el río river
robado stolen

robar v steal
el robo theft
la rodilla knee
rojo red
romántico romantic
romper v break
la ropa clothing; ~ **interior**
underwear
rosa pink
roto broken
el rubgy rugby
la rueda tire [tyre BE];
~ **pinchada** flat tire [tyre BE]
las ruinas ruins
la ruta route; ~ **de**
senderismo walking route

S

la sábana sheet
el sacacorchos corkscrew
el saco de dormir sleeping
bag
la sala room; ~ **de conciertos**
concert hall; ~ **de espera**
waiting room; ~ **de**
reuniones meeting room
la salida check-out (hotel)
la salida n exit; ~ **de urgencia**
emergency exit
las salidas departures
(airport)
salir v exit, leave
el salón room; ~ **de**
congresos convention hall;
~ **de juegos recreativos**

arcade; **~ de manicura** nail salon

¡Salud! Cheers!

la salud health

las sandalias sandals

sangrar v bleed

la sangre blood

el santuario shrine

la sartén frying pan

la sauna sauna

el secador de pelo hair dryer

la secreción discharge (bodily fluid)

la seda silk

sediento thirsty

la seguridad security

el seguro insurance

seguro safe (protected)

el sello n stamp (postage)

el semáforo traffic light

la semana week

semanal weekly

el seminario seminar

el sendero trail; **~ para bicicletas** bike route

el seno breast

sentarse v sit

separado separated (marriage)

ser v be

serio serious

el servicio restroom [toilet BE]; **~** service (in a restaurant); **~ completo** full-service; **~ de habitaciones** room service;

~ inalámbrico a internet wireless internet service; **~ de internet** internet service; **~ de lavandería** laundry service; **~ de limpieza de habitaciones** housekeeping service

la servilleta napkin

sí yes

el sida AIDS

la silla chair; **~ para niños** child seat; **~ de ruedas** wheelchair

el símbolo symbol (keyboard)

sin without; **~ alcohol** non-alcoholic; **~ grasa** fat free; **~ receta** over the counter (medication)

la sinagoga synagogue

el sitio de interés attraction (place)

el sobre envelope

el socorrista lifeguard

el sol sun

solamente only

soleado sunny

solo alone

soltero single (marriage)

el sombrero hat

la somnolencia drowsiness

sordo deaf

soso bland

el suavizante conditioner

el subtítulo subtitle

sucio dirty

la sudadera sweatshirt
el suelo floor
el sujetador bra
súper super (fuel)
superior upper
el supermercado grocery store, supermarket
la supervisión supervision
el sur south
el surfista windsurfer

T

la tabla board; ~ **de snowboard** snowboard; ~ **de surf** surfboard
la talla size; ~ **grande** plus size; ~ **pequeña** petite size
el taller garage (repair)
el talón de equipaje luggage [baggage BE] ticket
el tampón tampon
la taquilla locker; ~ reservation desk
tarde late (time)
la tarde afternoon
la tarjeta card; ~ **de cajero automático** ATM card; ~ **de crédito** credit card; ~ **de débito** debit card; ~ **de embarque** boarding pass; ~ **internacional de estudiante** international student card; ~ **de memoria** memory card; ~ **de negocios**

business card; ~ **postal** postcard; ~ **de seguro** insurance card; ~ **de socio** membership card; ~ **telefónica** phone card
la tasa fee
el taxi taxi
la taza cup; ~ **medidora** measuring cup
el teatro theater; ~ **de la ópera** opera house
la tela impermeable groundcloth [groundsheet BE]
el teleférico cable car
el teléfono telephone; ~ **móvil** cell [mobile BE] phone; ~ **público** pay phone
la telesilla chair lift
el telesquí ski/drag lift
la televisión TV
el templo temple (religious)
temprano early
el tenedor fork
tener v have; ~ **dolor** v hurt (have pain); ~ **náuseas** v be nauseous
el tenis tennis
la tensión arterial blood pressure
la terminal terminal (airport)
terminar v end
la terracotta terracotta
terrible terrible
el texto n text (message)

el tiempo time; ~ weather
la tienda store; ~ **de
alimentos naturales**
health food store;
~ **de antigüedades**
antique store; ~ **de
bebidas alcohólicas**
liquor store [off-licence
BE]; ~ **de campaña** tent;
~ **de deportes** sporting
goods store; ~ **de fotografía**
camera store; ~ **de juguetes**
toy store; ~ **de música**
music store; ~ **de recuerdos**
souvenir store; ~ **de regalos**
gift shop; ~ **de ropa** clothing
store
las tijeras scissors
la tintorería dry cleaner
el tipo de cambio exchange
rate
tirar v pull (door sign)
la tirita bandage
la toalla towel
la toallita baby wipe
el tobillo ankle
el torneo de golf golf
tournament
la torre tower
la tos n cough
toser v cough
el total total (amount)
trabajar v work
tradicional traditional
traducir v translate

traer v bring
tragar v swallow
el traje suit
tranquilo quiet
el tren train; ~ **rápido** express
train
triste sad
la trona highchair
el trozo piece
la tumbona deck chair
el turista tourist

U

último last
la universidad university
uno one
la uña nail; ~ **del dedo**
fingernail; ~ **del pie** toenail
urgente urgent
usar v use

V

las vacaciones vacation
[holiday BE]
vaciar v empty
la vacuna vaccination
la vagina vagina
la validez valid
valioso valuable
el valle valley
el valor value
el vaquero denim
los vaqueros jeans
el vaso glass (drinking)
el váter químico chemical

toilet
vegetariano vegetarian
la vejiga bladder
vender v sell
el veneno poison
venir v come
la ventana window
el ventilador fan (appliance)
ver v see
verde green
el vestido dress (piece of clothing)
el viaje trip
el vidrio glass (material)
viejo old
la viña vineyard
la violación n rape
violar v rape
el visado visa (passport document)
visitar v visit
la vitamina vitamin
la vitrina display case
viudo widowed
vivir v live
vomitar v vomit
el vuelo flight; ~ **internacional** international flight; ~ **nacional** domestic flight

la zona area; ~ **de compras** shopping area; ~ **de fumadores** smoking area; ~ **para picnic** picnic area
el zoológico zoo
zurcir v mend

Z

la zapatería shoe store
las zapatillas slippers; ~ **de deporte** sneaker
los zapatos shoes